The Ultimate Handfasting: *Unlock the Magic of Your Pagan Dream Wedding*

KAT STICKER

DEDICATION

To my beloved husband and eternal partner, Michael, whose radiant soul illuminates every corner of my life and with whom I have twice handfasted. With each handfasting, we have not only bound our hands but also intertwined our hearts, strengthening the unbreakable bond we share. Your unwavering love and support have been the guiding lights in my journey, inspiring every word I pen. This book is a testament to our enduring love and the beautiful journey we continue to share together.

CONTENTS

INTRODUCTION

Marriage is arguably the most important decision you will
make in your lifetime. The sacred union of two hearts lays
the foundation for family, generates expectations and creates
legal obligations. You want your committed relationship to
stand the test of time. Proclaiming this union to the world,
surrounded by the warmth and love of friends and family, is
a time of immense joy and celebration. Whether you have
desire and resources for a large or small event, you want
your ceremony to be meaningful, memorable and even
magical.

Are you concerned your special moment will not turn out to
be your dream wedding? Are you lost in the planning
process, unsure of how to add elements that reflect your
Pagan lifestyle or your true personality? Do you worry the
rituals you incorporate may fail to captivate your wedding
guests, leading them to perceive your wedding as cheesy,
boring, insincere or a parody of the sanctity of marriage? Are
you anxious your standard, off-the-shelf wedding might end
up feeling like an extravagant expenditure rather than the

best day of your life? By the end of this book, you will have mastered the skills needed to plan a meaningful, memorable, and magical handfasting.

Imagine a world where love knows no boundaries, where ancient traditions meet modern romance, and where the power of nature intertwines with the strength of your bond. Picture a scene where you and your partner stand under the canopy of majestic trees, your hands bound together with sacred cords, as you embark on a journey of love, unity, and enchantment. Welcome to the captivating realm of Pagan Handfasting, a world of mysticism, symbolism, and timeless rituals.

In this book, you'll step into the heart of these magical ceremonies, where the air is filled with the scent of wildflowers, the whispers of ancient chants, and the promise of eternal love. You'll meet couples whose love stories are as diverse as the stars in the night sky, yet united by a shared desire to celebrate their love in a way that's as unique as their connection. As you turn the pages, you'll be transported to ancient groves, moonlit gardens, and sacred circles where love reigns supreme. You'll witness the exchange of heartfelt vows infused with the wisdom of generations, the binding of hands symbolizing unbreakable love, and the casting of circles that protect and bless the union. Each ritual is a tapestry of emotions, a blend of tradition and personal expression, and a testament to the enduring power of love.

But this book is more than just a glimpse into the world of Pagan handfasting; it's your invitation to embark on your own enchanted journey. You'll discover practical guidance on planning and crafting your unique handfasting ceremony, from selecting meaningful symbols to choosing the perfect location. You'll learn about the rich history and symbolism behind each ritual, allowing you to infuse your celebration with depth and significance. Whether you're a couple seeking to celebrate your love in an authentic and enchanting way or simply an explorer of diverse traditions, this book is your key to unlocking the secrets of Pagan handfasting. Here is your passport to a world of unity, love, and magic transcending time and space.

So, are you ready to embark on a journey where love knows no limits, where tradition and innovation blend seamlessly, and where your love story becomes an enchanting epic? Let's get started in this book and let your love story unfold in the most extraordinary way.

Background

I have had the pleasure and opportunity to plan several wedding events over the years, including my own. My must-have requirements for my own wedding were:

- the ceremony must include some unique rituals;
- symbolic elements will be present that are meaningful to me and my partner;
- our children will have roles in the event and feel they are part of the big day; and
- the guests will have fun!

In the extensive research I conducted, I predominantly discovered traditional ceremony concepts rooted in American Christian customs. The bridal magazines, the bridal shows, the wedding stores and wedding planners all offered common-place, mainstream wedding plans. But I did not feel like a common-place bride. I did not want a cookie-cutter wedding. I craved something magical, Pagan, whimsical yet elegant, simple yet engaging. When I began researching non-American traditions, I found some interesting ideas.

Contemporary Pagan nuptials, known as handfasting, have their roots deeply embedded in a similar tradition that traces back to the Middle Ages and even further. Until the Reformation, numerous European cultures embraced the tradition of handfasting, which led to a legally binding engagement rather than the actual marriage ceremony. The word handfasting is equivalent to a handshake to seal a contract. In certain regions, handfasting marked the commencement of a trial marriage. Regardless of the context, this ritual was normally succeeded by a formal marriage ceremony.

In some cultures, handfasting was interpreted as a commitment that lasts "one year and a day." This specific duration is often seen as a trial period or a temporary commitment, after which the couple decides whether to continue their relationship and enter into a permanent marriage or part ways. This approach allows partners to experience a significant period of life together before making a lifelong commitment.

Today, handfasting has evolved into something different. It normally serves as the marriage ceremony itself rather than a trial run, but some of the past rituals remain. There is a specific ritual, also called handfasting, which binds the hands of the wedding couple with a sacred cord to symbolize their union. I incorporated some rituals from different cultures, including handfasting, into my wedding planning and created some of my own rituals. Being an artist and ritual designer, I chose to bring my vision to life.

My fear that the wedding guests would be confused or offended by my selection of ceremonial rituals was relieved when the guests turned out to be delighted and entertained by the distinctive choices. From the outset, I primed our guests for the unique experience awaiting them by incorporating our theme into the save-the-date cards and invitations. I chose to retain some traditional elements in the ceremony, such as the exchange of wedding rings and vows. However, these were not your typical rings and vows. They were meticulously tailored to align with my Pagan theme, adding a personal and distinctive touch to our special day. The feedback from our attendees has been overwhelmingly positive, affirming the success of our unique approach.

Pagan Roots

The interpretation of the term 'Pagan' has undergone significant evolution throughout the years. Historically, it referred to religious or spiritual practices and beliefs outside of the world's main religions. In modern times, it may be referred to as NeoPaganism, encompassing a resurgence of various eclectic religions.

Paganism is a broad category which often includes various polytheistic, nature-based, and earth-centered faiths. However, the majority of modern Pagans subscribe to the belief in the divine essence of the natural world, leading to

Paganism frequently being characterized as an Earth-centric religion.

This book does not aim to engage in a debate about the current definition of Paganism or NeoPaganism. If you identify as any type of Pagan and desire to incorporate Pagan rituals into your wedding ceremony, this book is specifically tailored to cater to your needs. Paganism is an umbrella term covering a wide range of beliefs and practices, and there is significant diversity within this community. As such, the beliefs and practices of one Pagan group or individual can be quite different from another's.

Traditions, Rituals and Ceremonies

Before we go further, let's talk about the terms ceremony, ritual and tradition as used in this book. *Rituals* are rites, customs or a series of actions in a particular order designed for a symbolic value or for an intention of transformation. An example of a common ritual is presenting a birthday cake with flaming candles to the birthday boy, the guests singing the "Happy Birthday" song, and the birthday boy making a wish and blowing out the candles. The intent is mark the passing of a year of life while wishing for something specific in the next year.

Rituals can be powerful catalysts! While some rituals may incorporate an element of magic, others do not. Rituals are often performed for certain important events or ceremonies and may be prescribed through tradition or religion.

In essence, *ceremonies* may be viewed as a tapestry of interconnected rituals. A ceremony is similar to a ritual, but I would consider it a more formal string of multiple rituals to mark an important occasion or for a particular purpose. Ceremonies normally involve multiple people, and everyone focusing their intentions on the same purpose can create powerful energy. They give us memorable milestones and allow us to share and celebrate important passages in our lives. Rituals and ceremonies are important because they help us to focus our intentions.

Traditions are deeply ingrained practices or beliefs lovingly handed down from one generation to the next. They frequently encompass shared celebrations. These traditions can be cultural, religious, or unique to a particular family, each with its own distinct flavor and significance. By observing these traditions, individuals not only honor their heritage but also fortify the sense of community among participants, thereby fostering a stronger bond and mutual understanding.

Traditions can be important in the context of rituals. Traditions and rituals serve as a link to our past and a bridge to our future. They are significant because they cultivate a sense of identity, continuity and belonging. They create a shared experience and a common bond among those who participate in them.

Let's consider an illustrative family, the Smiths. Every year, the Smith family eagerly awaits the arrival of winter. Not just for the snow and the holidays, but for their annual tradition of baking cookies. This tradition began with their great-grandmother, who was known for her delicious cookies. She used to bake them every winter, and the smell would fill the entire house, bringing everyone together. Her recipe, a well-guarded secret, was passed down to each generation. Now, although she's no longer with them, they continue this tradition. The act of baking these cookies every winter strengthens their familial bond, reconnects them with their past, and brings a sense of continuity and comfort.

The same family, the Smiths, also have a specific ritual they follow on New Year's Eve. As the clock strikes midnight, they gather in a circle, each holding a small piece of paper where they've written something they want to leave behind from the old year. One by one, they throw these papers into a fire. This ritual, for them, symbolizes the release of old burdens and the welcoming of new beginnings. It's a symbolic act helping them express their hopes and intentions for the new year.

In this story, the Smiths' cookie-baking activity is a tradition, a customary practice passed down through generations, bringing them together and strengthening their sense of identity. On the other hand, their New Year's Eve paper-burning activity is a ritual, a symbolic action that serves to convey a profound meaning and transformation, in this case, the release of the old and the welcoming of the new.

Traditions and rituals often intertwine, with rituals potentially evolving into traditions over time. Despite their overlap, they each serve distinct purposes. Traditions primarily cultivate a sense of belonging and identity, acting as a unifying thread which binds a community or group together. However, rituals carry a more symbolic and transformative role, providing a deeper, often spiritual, meaning to our actions.

Handfasting ceremonies (composed of several rituals) are a time-honored tradition, which has gracefully evolved over the centuries, adapting to the modern era while retaining its rich historical roots. Originating from practical necessities and ancient laws, it is imbued with profound rituals carrying deep significance. However, these rituals are often overlooked or taken for granted as mere traditions, with their original intent and symbolism lost in translation. This book aims to enlighten you about the true essence of these rituals, empowering you to create your own meaningful ceremonies that could potentially become cherished traditions in the future.

Purpose of the Book

This book is designed to make it easier for you to plan a memorable, Pagan-style handfasting event, customized to suit your preferences. All parts of the pre- and post-handfasting events can be ritualistic, not only the handfasting ceremony. You can have confidence the magical rituals included will be effective. The handfasting events will be meaningful for the couple and the guests through symbolism customized for the couple. Your guests will be impressed and have fun and may participate in certain rituals if desired. Your handfasting will be recognizable as a Pagan-style wedding; however, you can still include mainstream traditions as well.

I wrote this book to ease the burden on my fellow Pagan handfasting celebrants by providing a guide on how to design handfasting rituals that have deep-seated personal meaning and will add value to your special day. In the chapters to come, we will explore rituals in modern Pagan handfasting that you may want to incorporate into your handfasting. I provide an extensive selection of contemporary Pagan handfasting traditions for you to choose from. Furthermore, I have meticulously crafted a series of non-traditional rituals for your consideration, adding a distinctive touch to your special day or the events leading to ceremony. Some rituals can be added to any style ceremony. All can be further customized. If you're in pursuit of the ultimate Pagan handfasting, then you're in the right place. Continue reading to discover how you can craft your own flawless ceremony. I've meticulously prepared templates for free download from my website to assist you in planning the rituals and sequencing the events, along with a comprehensive event checklist.

In Part 1, we will embark on an enlightening journey exploring the rich tapestry of customary rituals from diverse cultures. Part 2 examines the time-honored traditions of NeoPagan rituals and distinctive rituals, which will add a touch of sparkle to your ceremony. Chapter 9 provides instructions on how to personalize any of the rituals you opt for, tailoring them to your unique preferences and needs. Part 3 covers the comprehensive process of assembling your unique handfasting chain of events. We will thoroughly explore all the potential event alternatives, the sequence of events and provide additional guidance to ensure everything proceeds seamlessly.

After each ritual mentioned, there is a 3-pronged key featuring:

- *Good fit for*: lists the events best suited for the ritual
- *Children or extended family participation*: Suitable or not suitable
- *Complexity*: Easy, Medium or Advanced

Complexity may be marked as medium or advanced if it requires additional effort, specialized skill or knowledge or access to certain land features or tools, which may be difficult to find or expensive to obtain.

Thank you for choosing to purchase the book. I wholeheartedly wish you the best of luck on your exciting journey ahead. May peace, love, and harmony envelop you and your partner, Now go create a stunning handfasting event and a marriage filled with unending bliss.

PART 1
EMBRACING PAGAN
HANDFASTING TRADITIONS

CHAPTER 1 COMMON THREADS

The Peculiar Union

Once upon a time in a picturesque little town nestled among rolling hills, there lived a couple whose love story was as unique as the setting itself. Maria and Thomas were free spirits who had chosen to embark on an extraordinary adventure together: a handfasting ceremony. As their marriage date approached, the excitement in the community was palpable. Word had spread that Maria and Thomas were planning a one-of-a-kind celebration, and the entire community was buzzing with curiosity. People couldn't help but wonder what kind of ceremony the couple had in store.

The day arrived, and the sun bathed the town in its golden glow. The ceremony was set in a lush meadow surrounded by ancient oak trees, a serene natural cathedral. Friends and family gathered, and the air was filled with a sense of wonder and expectation.

The couple, dressed in flowing, earthy attire, stood before an intricately woven handfasting cord, its colors representing their individual journeys now intertwined. The officiant, a wise old woman known for her deep connection to nature, began the ceremony with a warm smile.

"Have you ever found yourself at a wedding or watched one unfold in a film yet felt unsure about what was transpiring before your eyes?" she asked, her voice carrying a hint of mischief.

The guests exchanged puzzled glances but leaned in attentively. A murmur rippled through the crowd.

"This is because weddings and handfastings, despite their cultural and temporal variations, share certain recognizable elements," she explained. "While the sequence and execution of these rituals can differ, their presence can be identifiable." Guests began to murmur in understanding.

"Our intention is what matters," she went on. "When we keep the focus on love and commitment at the center, the deepest meaning can be conveyed."

Maria and Thomas exchanged mischievous glances, knowing their ceremony would be anything but ordinary.

As the officiant began to describe the first ritual, a gentle breeze rustled through the trees. The couple seized the opportunity and unfurled a large, vibrant tapestry. Instead of lighting a unity candle, they unveiled a stunning mosaic of stained glass, casting a kaleidoscope of colors across the meadow.

Guests gasped in awe at the unexpected beauty before them.

The ceremony continued with laughter and love; each expected ritual replaced with something utterly surprising. Instead of exchanging traditional vows, Maria and Thomas sang a duet under the dappled sunlight, their voices harmonizing like a love song composed by the universe itself. Instead of exchanging rings, Maria and Thomas exchanged wooden figures, which they had hand-carved with an engraving of symbols of their love for one another.

As the ceremony came to a close, the officiant looked out at the beaming guests. "Just be prepared for questions from your guests as to why expected traditional elements are absent," she teased.

And indeed, there were questions, but they were questions of wonder and delight. As the guests left the meadow, they couldn't help but marvel at the unique love story they had witnessed that day.

Maria and Thomas' handfasting had been a testament to the beauty of forging one's path, creating rituals that celebrated their love in a way uniquely their own. And in the picturesque town, under the ancient oaks, they had shared a truly unforgettable wedding, proving love, like life, was an adventure meant to be embraced with open hearts and open minds.

Common Handfasting Rituals

Have you ever found yourself at a wedding or watched one unfold in a film, yet felt unsure about what was happening?

This is unlikely because weddings and handfastings, despite their cultural and temporal variations, share certain recognizable elements. This chapter delves into several rituals, which are almost invariably incorporated in some form into Pagan handfastings. While the sequence and execution of these rituals can differ, their presence can be identifiable. However, this doesn't mean you can't orchestrate a wholly unique event without one or more of these common or expected rituals. Remember, this is a buffet of options. Make sure you identify your intention for including each ritual.

While a wedding holds some entertainment value, the purpose of the handfasting is to bind two souls together in a lifetime of a committed relationship. That should clearly be the focus. Otherwise, it can be off-putting to some guests if an elaborate ritual appears to only be for the purpose of showmanship.

As the following handfasting rituals span across cultures, **they will not be repeated in chapters 2-8 unless there is a unique spin on it in that culture's practice**. Cultural variations within Paganism can influence the details of how these rituals are performed.

1. Officiant Blesses Couple and Proceedings:
In a Pagan handfasting ceremony, the officiant plays a crucial role in setting the spiritual and sacred tone of the event. They may invoke blessings from deities of the couple's choice, call upon the elements, ancestors of the couple or connect with the natural world to seek blessings for the couple's union. This part of the ceremony serves to

create a sacred and ceremonial space. It aligns the couple and the gathering with the energies of the earth and cosmos.

- *Good fit for: Engagement Ceremony, Handfasting Ceremony, House Blessing*
- *Children or extended family participation: Suitable to the extent that the couple wants the Officiant to bless them and their children*
- *Complexity: Easy to medium*

2. Marriage Vows:
Pagan handfasting ceremonies often emphasize personal and heartfelt vows exchanged between the couple. These vows are often a reflection of the couple's love, commitment, and shared values. They may include promises to honor and support each other, to celebrate life's joys and face its challenges together, and to maintain a spiritual connection. Pagan couples often draw inspiration from nature, mythology, or their own spiritual beliefs when crafting their vows.

- *Good fit for: Engagement Ceremony, Handfasting Ceremony*
- *Children or extended family participation: Not Suitable*
- *Complexity: Easy to medium*

3. Handfasting:
The handfasting ritual in a Pagan ceremony symbolizes the physical and spiritual union of the couple. Traditionally, the couple's hands are bound together with a cord, ribbon or other type of cloth in a figure-eight or infinity symbol. This cord is often made of natural materials, such as silk, cotton, or hemp, and is often chosen for its symbolic colors. It can be

personalized for theme of the event. For instance, a Viking themed handfasting may use a cord made from **natural materials like twine, leather, or fabric. This cord could be adorned with symbols or runes holding particular significance for the couple or their community.**

The act of binding the hands of the couple represents the eternal nature of their commitment, the interconnectedness of their lives, and their journey together as partners in the sacred circle of life.

Historically the handfasting cord ritual was completed to signify the engagement commitment, not the marriage. The handfasting ceremony is believed to have originated from ancient Celtic traditions, where it was used as a form of betrothal. The term "handfasting" is derived from the Old Norse "hand-festa," which means "to strike a bargain by joining hands." The couple would join their hands together, and a cord or ribbon would be wrapped around them, symbolizing their pledge to each other.

After the ceremony, the handfasting cord is often kept as a memento of the couple's commitment. Some couples choose to display it in their home, while others may choose to keep it in a special box or other container. In modern times, handfasting ceremonies are often incorporated into wedding ceremonies to honor cultural heritage or to add a unique and personal touch. It can be performed by a religious officiant, a celebrant, or a close friend or family member.

- *Good fit for: Engagement Ceremony, Handfasting Ceremony*
- *Children or extended family participation: Suitable*

- *Complexity: Easy*

4. *Exchange of Rings*:
Rings exchanged during a Pagan handfasting ceremony often hold symbolic significance. The circle of the ring represents eternity and the unending nature of love, while the choice of materials and any inscriptions can be meaningful to the couple. This exchange reaffirms the commitment made in the vows and signifies the eternal nature of their union.

- *Good fit for: Engagement Ceremony, Handfasting Ceremony*
- *Children or extended family participation: Not Suitable*
- *Complexity: Easy*

5. *Unity Ritual*:
Many Pagan handfasting ceremonies include a unity ritual symbolizing the merging of two lives into one. This could involve lighting a central unity candle, blending two containers of earth, water, or salt, or sharing a symbolic meal or drink together. These rituals emphasize the couple's shared journey and their connection to the natural world and the divine.

The unity candle ceremony is an Irish tradition connected to the element of fire. The two outer candles symbolize the respective families of the bride and groom, while the third candle, once lit, represents the formation of their new, united family.

The lighting of the unity candle is a relatively recent addition to traditional wedding ceremonies and is more common in modern, Western handfastings and weddings. It is a symbolic conclusion to the process of the joining of two families and signifies that the bride and the groom have not only joined as a couple but also as a family.

Another common way to light the candles is the mothers of the bride and groom light the two outer candles at the beginning of the wedding. Later in the ceremony, the bride and groom use these two flames to light the third candle together, symbolizing the joining of their two families into one. The unity candle can also symbolize the joining together of two individuals, becoming one in commitment. The taper candles are lit by representatives from each family to symbolize the love and allegiance that each family has for either the bride or the groom.

- *Good fit for: Engagement Ceremony, Engagement Party, Family Engagement Dinner, Handfasting Ceremony, Reception*
- *Children or extended family participation: Suitable*
- *Complexity: Easy to medium*

6. Pronouncement of Marriage:
Following the vows, handfasting, and ring exchange, the officiant formally pronounces the couple as married. This declaration is a sacred moment, signifying the culmination of the rituals and the couple's spiritual union. It acknowledges they are now bound together as partners in love and in their shared spiritual path. As in mainstream weddings, the couple may kiss their first kiss as a married couple.

- *Good fit for: Handfasting Ceremony*

- *Children or extended family participation: Suitable to the extent the couple wants the officiant to pronounce their marriage and unity as a family*
- *Complexity: Easy*

7. Celebration with Guests:
The reception may contain several meaningful rituals. After the formal pronouncement, the couple and their guests often celebrate in a festive and communal manner. This may include dancing, feasting, music, and other activities that bring joy and merriment to the occasion. It's a time for the couple to express gratitude to their community for their support and to celebrate their union with those they hold dear.

- *Good fit for: Engagement Party, Family Engagement Dinner, Bridal Shower, Bachelorette Party, Bachelor Party, Rehearsal Dinner, Reception*
- *Children or extended family participation: Suitable*
- *Complexity: Easy to Advanced*

Differences Between Pagan Weddings and Mainstream Christian Weddings

While we cannot cover every wedding style from all religions in this book, I will provide a brief contrast between Pagan and Christian wedding ceremonies. This clarifies the difference between Pagan style weddings and the mainstream weddings pushed at western bridal shows and in wedding magazines. Pagan handfasting ceremonies and traditional Christian weddings, while both celebrating the union of a couple, have distinct differences rooted in their respective spiritual and cultural traditions. Here's a comparison of key elements:

1. Ceremony Setting:

- Pagan Handfasting: Often held outdoors in natural settings like forests, meadows, or near bodies of water, emphasizing the connection to nature.
- Christian Weddings: Typically held in churches or chapels, symbolizing the presence and blessing of God within a sacred space.

2. Spiritual Beliefs and Symbols

- Pagan Handfasting: Incorporates elements and directions, nature symbolism, and can involve various deities from different pantheons. Ritual tools like candles, crystals, and wands are common.
- Christian Weddings: Focus on Christian symbolism, such as the cross, and center around the blessings and teachings of Christianity. Religious texts and prayers are integral parts.

3. Ceremony Structure and Rituals

- Pagan Handfasting: Features the handfasting ritual (tying of hands), casting a circle, and may include unique rituals like jumping the broom.
- Christian Weddings: Includes the exchange of vows and rings, readings from the Bible, and often a sermon or homily by a minister.
- Both may have include unity rituals.

4. Officiants

- Pagan Handfasting: Led by someone significant to the couple's spiritual path, like a High Priestess or Priest, Druid, or an ordained friend or family member.
- Christian Weddings: Typically conducted by a Christian minister, priest, or pastor authorized by the church.

5. Vows and Commitment

- Pagan Handfasting: Vows are often personalized, written by the couple and focused on equality, with flexibility in the length and type of commitment (e.g., "a year and a day," a lifetime, or eternity).
- Christian Weddings: Vows are traditionally based on Christian teachings, focusing on lifelong commitment, with phrases like "till death do us part."

6. Legal Recognition

- Pagan Handfasting: May require legal measures separate from the ceremony to be recognized by the state, depending on local laws.
- Christian Weddings: Typically legally recognized, with the officiant often authorized to sign the marriage license.

Both types of ceremonies celebrate love and commitment but do so through the lens of their respective spiritual beliefs and cultural traditions, reflecting the values and practices of their communities.

FAQs about Pagan Handfastings

Addressing common questions and misconceptions about Pagan handfastings can help provide a clearer understanding of these ceremonies.

1. Is Handfasting Legally Binding?

 The legal status of a handfasting depends on the laws of the region where it's performed. In many places, a separate civil ceremony or legal paperwork is required for the union to be legally recognized. The handfasting itself is primarily a spiritual or symbolic commitment.

2. Do All Pagans Practice Handfasting?

Not all Pagans participate in handfasting ceremonies. Paganism encompasses a wide range of beliefs and practices, and not every tradition includes handfasting. It's a choice made by individual couples based on their beliefs and preferences.

3. Is Handfasting a Form of Marriage?

Handfasting is often akin to marriage in its symbolism of union and commitment, but it's distinct in its practices and meanings. Some view it as a form of spiritual marriage, while others see it as a commitment ceremony that may or may not be equivalent to a traditional marriage.

4. Are Handfastings Only for Wiccans or Druids?

While handfasting is commonly associated with Wiccan and Druidic traditions, it's not exclusive to them. Various Pagan paths practice handfasting, and it can be adapted to suit the spiritual beliefs of any Pagan couple.

5. Can Anyone Have a Handfasting Ceremony?

Yes, anyone who feels aligned with the values and symbolism of handfasting can choose to have such a ceremony. It's about personal belief and connection to the rituals involved, rather than belonging to a specific religious group.

6. Is Handfasting a 'Year and a Day' Commitment?

The "year and a day" term is traditional in some Pagan paths, but it's not a rule. Couples can choose the length of their commitment, whether it's for a year and a day, a lifetime, or any other duration holding personal significance. It is important to check the legal requirements in your locality and potentially consult legal counsel. If you are legally wed, you may not be able to easily dissolve a marriage after a year and a day.

7. Does Handfasting Involve Witchcraft or Magic?

While some handfasting ceremonies might include elements that could be considered magical or witchcraft-related, especially in Wiccan contexts, the ceremony itself is not inherently about performing magic. It's a ritual of commitment and can be as spiritual or secular as the couple desires.

8. Are Handfastings Inclusive of LGBTQ+ Couples?

The Pagan community is generally inclusive, and handfasting ceremonies often reflect this inclusivity. Many Pagan paths and traditions welcome and celebrate unions of all couples, regardless of gender or sexual orientation.

9. Do You Need to Be Initiated into a Pagan Path to Have a Handfasting?

No, initiation into a specific Pagan path is not a prerequisite for a handfasting ceremony. While some couples may choose to incorporate specific traditions from their spiritual path, the ceremony can be personalized to reflect the beliefs and preferences of each individual couple.

10. Is a Handfasting Ceremony Always Performed by a Pagan Priest or Priestess?

A handfasting can be led by a Pagan priest or priestess, but it's not a strict requirement. Some couples prefer to have a friend, family member, or a legally ordained officiant who understands and respects their beliefs to conduct the ceremony. It is important to check the legal requirements in your locality to ensure your officiant is able to perform a binding nuptial.

Understanding these aspects of handfasting helps in appreciating the diversity and personalization characterizing these ceremonies within the Pagan community.

Recommended Additional Reading:

"Paganism: Pagan holidays, beliefs, gods and goddesses, symbols, rituals, practices, and much more! An Introductory Guide" by Riley Star

CHAPTER 2 UK /CELTIC HANDFASTING TRADITIONS

A Celtic Love Story

Amidst the lush emerald hills of the Celtic countryside, a couple, Eilidh and Ciaran, had decided to embark on a journey of love steeped in tradition and symbolism. Their love story was as timeless as the rolling hills, and their handfasting ceremony would be a celebration of their connection to their Celtic roots.

The ceremony took place on a crisp autumn day, beneath the sprawling branches of an ancient oak tree, its leaves painted in shades of amber and gold. The air was filled with the soft melodies of Celtic harp music, played by a dear friend. Friends and family from the village had gathered, their presence a testament to the strength of community bonds. Eilidh, adorned in a flowing gown adorned with intricate Celtic knotwork, stood with Ciaran, who wore a kilt woven in the colors of their clan. At the heart of the ceremony lay the handfasting cord, a finely woven ribbon representing their shared journey.

Their officiant, a Druid steeped in Celtic tradition, began by invoking the elements. With reverence, they called upon Earth, Air, Fire, and Water, symbolizing the foundational elements of life and the sacred balance within nature. The couple stood on a circle of stones, each one representing a point of the compass, aligning them with the rhythms of the Earth. With grace and humility, Eilidh and Ciaran extended their hands towards each other, ready to embark on this momentous journey together. The handfasting cord, vibrant with colors mirroring the landscape, was placed around their bound hands. The Druid officiant explained the symbolism of the cord, emphasizing that it represented the interwoven threads of their lives and their commitment to walk this path together.

As the couple exchanged vows, they made promises to honor the elements, cherish the wisdom of their ancestors, and celebrate the seasons of life. The knot was tied, forming an intricate Celtic knotwork pattern, signifying the eternal nature of their love. Friends and family looked on, their faces reflecting the depth of emotion in the ceremony.

Following the exchange of vows, the couple lit a ceremonial bonfire. Its flames reached high into the sky, symbolizing the fire of their passion and the warmth of their love. They made offerings to the flames, a tribute to their ancestors and a gesture of gratitude for the blessings bestowed upon their union.

The celebration continued with a feast, where villagers shared dishes made from the bounties of the land and the sea. Music and dance filled the air, bringing a sense of joy and unity to the gathering. As the sun set behind the hills, casting a warm golden hue on the landscape, Eilidh and Ciaran's handfasting ceremony had not only united their hearts but had also strengthened their connection to the rich Celtic traditions, which had shaped their love story. They knew that their love, like the Celtic knot, was eternal and bound by the threads of history, community, and nature.

Eilidh and Ciaran's handfasting ceremony embodied the timeless traditions of the British Isles and Celtic regions, blending nature, community, and symbolism to create a profoundly meaningful celebration of love.

The Scope of UK Traditions

England, Wales, Ireland and Scotland share in many similar cultural traditions such as tying the knot with the handfasting cord and exchanging vows. Their handfasting ceremonies mainly encourage community involvement. Loved ones, including friends and family, are often invited to bear witness to the ceremony, extending their blessings and good wishes to the couple. This communal participation emphasizes the crucial role of love and support from one's community in the journey of marriage. After the ceremony, it's customary to have a feast or celebration where the community gathers to share food, drink, music, and dance. This festive atmosphere adds joy and merriment to the occasion.

British and Celtic Rituals

The handfasting traditions of both British and Celtic cultures are entrenched in their respective histories and cultures, presenting a vibrant mosaic of rituals and symbolic gestures. Celtic customs frequently synchronize handfasting ceremonies with particular seasons or celestial occurrences, such as solstices or equinoxes. These chosen dates bear unique significance and are often selected to symbolize the couple's pledge to each other. Some ancient Celtic weddings took place near ring forts, circular structures believed to have protective and symbolic properties. Couples would exchange vows within these forts. In ancient Celtic societies, dowries were common, and they often included valuable items like livestock or land. The exchange of dowries was a significant part of Celtic weddings.

Various symbols, such as Celtic knots, spirals, and triskeles, were incorporated into Celtic wedding rituals and decorations to represent concepts like eternity, unity, and the cycles of life. These ceremonies often incorporate intricate knotwork patterns, which symbolize the eternal nature of love and the interconnectedness of life. Celtic knotwork can be incorporated into many handfasting elements including the handfasting cord, wedding rings and other jewelry, invitations, ceremony décor, wedding attire, wedding favors, and cake decoration.

Druidic traditions have influenced Celtic handfasting ceremonies, emphasizing a connection to nature, the cycles of the seasons, and the importance of harmony with the environment. Druids may officiate the ceremony and invoke nature's elements and spirits.

More modern Irish weddings have traditions as well, which are not necessarily Pagan or religious. The Claddagh ring is a popular symbol of Irish love and friendship. The Claddagh features two hands holding a heart with a crown, symbolizing love, loyalty, and friendship. These rings are often exchanged as engagement or wedding rings. The Claddagh ring is not directly related to either Christian or Pagan tradition; rather, it has its origins in Irish folklore and history. The ring is named after the Claddagh, a fishing village in Galway, Ireland, where it is believed to have been created.

Horseshoes are a symbol of good luck in Irish culture. Brides may carry a small horseshoe as part of their bouquet or receive one as a gift.

Here are some key traditional rituals associated with British and Celtic handfasting ceremonies:

1. Elemental Invocations
In Celtic traditions, it's common to invoke the elements (Earth, Air, Fire, Water) during the ceremony. The invocations connect the couple to nature and represent balance and harmony in their union. The ceremony normally begins with the invocation of the Earth element, symbolizing stability, fertility, and prosperity. The couple may stand barefoot on the ground, symbolizing their connection to the Earth. They may also exchange rings made of natural materials, such as wood or stone, to further symbolize this connection. Next, the Air element is invoked, symbolizing

communication, intellect, and the breath of life. The Fire element is then invoked, symbolizing passion, transformation, and the spark of life. The couple may light a unity candle or a bonfire, symbolizing the passion and warmth of their love. They may also exchange rings of gold or other precious metals, symbolizing the transformative power of their union. Finally, the Water element is invoked, symbolizing emotion, intuition, and the flow of life. The couple may pour water into a shared vessel, symbolizing the blending of their emotions and the flow of their lives together.

- *Good fit for: All ceremonies or ceremonial rituals, Handfasting Ceremony*
- *Children or extended family participation: Suitable*
- *Complexity: Medium*

2. Ancestral Tributes

Some Celtic handfasting ceremonies pay tribute to ancestors by acknowledging their presence or invoking their blessings. This can be done through the lighting of candles, offering libations, or reciting ancestral prayers. Honoring ancestors as part of the ceremony can be done in several ways:

a. Lighting of Candles: The couple may light a candle in honor of their ancestors. This is often done at the beginning of the ceremony, symbolizing the presence of the ancestors and their guidance and protection.

b. Offering Libations: The couple may pour a drink (often mead, wine, or ale) into a special vessel, known as a quaich, and then pour it onto the ground or into a body of water as an offering to their ancestors. This is a way of sharing the celebration with those who have passed on.

c. Reciting Ancestral Prayers: The couple or the officiant may recite prayers or blessings which have been passed down through their family or cultural tradition. These prayers often ask for the ancestors' blessings and guidance in the couple's new life together.

d. Ancestor Altar: Some couples choose to set up a small altar or table with photos, mementos, or symbols representing their ancestors. This serves as a physical reminder of their ancestors' presence and influence in their lives.

e. Moment of Silence: A moment of silence can be observed during the ceremony to honor the ancestors. This is a time for reflection and remembrance.

These practices are not only a way to honor the ancestors but also a way to connect with the past and bring its wisdom and strength into the present. They add a deeper spiritual dimension to the handfasting ceremony, making it a truly unique and meaningful experience.

- *Good fit for: Family Engagement Dinner, Handfasting Ceremony*
- *Children or extended family participation: Suitable*
- *Complexity: Easy to medium*

3. *Exchange of Rings or Tokens*

British and Celtic handfasting ceremonies may include the exchange of symbolic tokens or gifts, such as coins, rings, or herbs. These tokens represent the couple's commitment and are often chosen for their cultural or personal significance. These tokens can take many forms, depending on the couple's personal preferences and cultural traditions. Here are a few examples:

a. Coins: Coins are often used as a symbol of prosperity and good fortune. The couple may exchange coins as a promise to provide for each other.

b. Rings: Rings are a universal symbol of commitment and love. In a handfasting ceremony, the exchange of rings can symbolize the couple's eternal bond.

c. Herbs: Certain herbs have specific meanings in Celtic tradition. For example, rosemary symbolizes remembrance, love, and loyalty, while lavender represents devotion and virtue. The couple may exchange herbs as a symbol of these qualities.

d. Stones or Crystals: In some ceremonies, couples may exchange stones or crystals having special significance. For example, a quartz crystal might symbolize clarity and balance in their relationship.

e. Handwritten Vows or Letters: Some couples choose to write personal vows or letters to each other, which they exchange during the ceremony. These can serve as a personal token of their commitment.

f. Family Heirlooms: If there are family heirlooms or other items of sentimental value, these can also be exchanged as tokens during a handfasting ceremony.

The specific tokens used in a handfasting ceremony can vary widely, depending on the couple's personal beliefs and cultural traditions. However, the underlying theme is always the same: these tokens are a physical representation of the couple's commitment to each other.

- *Good fit for: Proposal, Engagement Party, Family Engagement Dinner, Handfasting Ceremony, Reception*
- *Children or extended family participation: Suitable*
- *Complexity: Easy*

4. Blessings and Prayers

Blessings and prayers are an integral part of both British and Celtic handfasting ceremonies. They invoke divine or spiritual blessings for the couple's happiness, prosperity, and enduring love. The officiant may say a prayer or blessing, asking for divine guidance and protection for the couple. This can be a traditional prayer or a personalized one, depending on the couple's beliefs and preferences. The officiant may also say a blessing in Gaelic, the traditional language of the Celts. This blessing may ask for the couple's love to be as enduring as the hills and as deep as the sea.

Celtic spirituality often has a strong connection to the land and a reverence for the ancestors. Couples may seek blessings from the spirits of the land they are on, asking for guidance and protection. They may also invoke the blessings and wisdom of their Celtic ancestors, seeking their presence and support. The sun and moon are significant celestial bodies in Celtic spirituality. Couples may request blessings from these sources of light and energy to bring warmth, illumination, and balance into their marriage.

Celtic traditions have various nature deities associated with different aspects of the natural world. For example:

- Cernunnos: The Horned God of the Celts, associated with the wilderness, fertility, and the cycle of life and death.

- Danu: A mother goddess symbolizing the earth and fertility.

- Brigid: A triple goddess associated with healing, poetry, and craftsmanship.

Celtic spirituality is highly individualized, and the deities and blessings invoked in a handfasting ceremony should align with the couple's beliefs and practices.

- *Good fit for: all events associated with Handfasting*
- *Children or extended family participation: Suitable*
- *Complexity: Easy to Advanced*

5. *Perforated Stones*

Large stones with holes near the top were associated with healing, oaths and marriage customs in medieval and post-medieval Ireland. In some regions of Ireland, couples would incorporate the holed stone into their wedding ceremony. During the ritual, the couple would clasp hands through the hole, symbolizing their union and the binding of their love. This act was often accompanied by spoken vows and blessings. These stones, known as "marriage stones" or "oath stones," were believed to possess magical properties. The hole in the stone was seen as a gateway or portal to the spirit world, and by passing their hands through it, the couple was believed to be invoking the spirits' blessings on their union.

- *Good fit for: Proposal, Engagement Party, Handfasting Ceremony*
- *Children or extended family participation: Not suitable/couple only*
- *Complexity: Advanced*

These traditions, rooted in the rich history and folklore of the British Isles and Celtic regions, add depth and meaning to handfasting ceremonies. Couples often choose elements from these traditions to create a unique and personalized ceremony resonating with their beliefs and values.

Wales Tradition

Not repeating any common rituals stated above, here is a ritual prevalent in the tradition of Wales.

1. Besom Weddings

In Wales, the Roma community had their own unique way of solemnizing marriages, distinct from the church's recognition. They celebrated what were known as "Besom Weddings," a reference to a specific type of broom. In these unconventional ceremonies, couples would take a symbolic leap into matrimony by leaping over the broomstick without making physical contact with it. Interestingly, to dissolve their union, couples would perform a reverse leap over the broomstick, marking the end of their partnership.

The Besom Wedding was a significant part of the Roma community's culture and tradition. The broomstick, or besom, was a symbol of domesticity and the home. By leaping over it, the couple was symbolically crossing the threshold into their new life together.

The ceremony was usually held outdoors, often in the presence of family and friends. The couple would hold hands and jump over the broomstick together, signifying their commitment to each other and their willingness to face life's challenges together. The broomstick was decorated with flowers and ribbons, and sometimes painted in bright colors. The couple would often keep the broomstick as a memento of their wedding day. In some cases, the broomstick would be hung in the couple's home as a reminder of their vows and the commitment they made to each other.

- *Good fit for: Handfasting Ceremony*
- *Children or extended family participation: Not suitable/couple only*
- *Complexity: Easy*

Scottish Rituals

Not repeating any common rituals stated above, here are some rituals prevalent in Scottish tradition.

1. Jury Stone

Jury Stone, a cherished Scottish tradition, draws its strength from the ancestral legacy and the unique environment in which it takes place. The stone, a symbol of the past and the very essence of the Earth, holds deep significance. As the couple, representing the present moment, exchange their vows, they hold the stone together, symbolizing their unity. At the ceremony's conclusion, the stone finds its destiny either in the flowing waters of a river, representing the journey of life, or in the couple's garden, serving as a tangible and enduring reminder of their sacred vows. The river may be chosen to symbolize flow and change in their relationship over time, connection to nature or letting go of limitations and past burdens as the river carries them away. The garden may be chosen to symbolize growth and nurturing, personal and lasting connections or foundation and stability as it is a stable and enduring place. It is a personal preference where to release it.

The Jury Stone tradition is a testament to the enduring power of love and commitment, and the deep connection between humans and the natural world. The stone, often chosen for its unique shape or color, is a physical representation of the couple's bond. It is a symbol of their shared history and their shared future, a tangible reminder of the promises they have made to each other. The ceremony itself is simple, yet profound. The couple holds the stone together as they recite their vows, their hands touching both the stone and each other. This act symbolizes their unity, their shared strength, and their commitment to support each other through life's challenges.

- *Good fit for: Handfasting Ceremony, Honeymoon, House Blessing*
- *Children or extended family participation: Suitable*
- *Complexity: Easy*

2. Oathing Stone

Some Scottish couples choose to perform the handfasting ceremony over a large stone or rock, particularly if they have a special connection to a particular location. This stone is believed to absorb the energy and blessings of the ceremony. The use of a stone or rock in the handfasting ceremony is a unique Scottish tradition. The stone is often chosen for its significance to the couple, such as a stone from a place they love or a place which holds special memories for them. The stone is placed in the center of the ceremony, and the couple stands over it as they perform the handfasting with a cord or ribbon. After the ceremony, the couple may choose to keep the stone as a memento of their special day, or they may return it to the place where it was found, leaving a piece of their love and commitment in that special location.

- *Good fit for: Handfasting Ceremony*
- *Children or extended family participation: Not suitable/couple only*
- *Complexity: Easy*

3. The Quaich Ceremony

The Quaich is a two-handled, shallow drinking cup traditionally used in Scotland to offer a drink to welcome guests. In some ceremonies, the couple may sip from the Quaich together, symbolizing their shared journey. A Quaich filled with whisky is passed around to the guests for a toast to the couple's happiness and prosperity. The Quaich, pronounced "quake", is derived from the Gaelic word "cuach", which means cup. It can be made of wood, pewter, silver, or gold, and is often engraved with Celtic designs or family crests. The two handles, or "lugs", are designed to be held with both hands, symbolizing trust between the giver and the receiver.

The Quaich has a rich history in Scotland, dating back to the 17th century. It was originally used by clans to welcome guests to their lands and to offer a drink of friendship. It was also used in traditional Scottish weddings, where the bride and groom would both drink from the Quaich to symbolize their bond and shared future. Today, the Quaich is still used in many Scottish ceremonies, including weddings, christenings, and Burns Night celebrations. It is also a popular gift for special occasions, such as birthdays, retirements, and anniversaries. The Quaich is a symbol of Scottish hospitality and friendship and is a cherished part of Scotland's cultural heritage.

- *Good fit for: Handfasting Ceremony*
- *Children or extended family participation: Not suitable for children unless non-alcoholic*
- *Complexity: Easy*

4. The Creeling of the Bride and Groom
In some Scottish regions, it was customary to "creel" the bride and groom. A creel is a type of basket, and the newlyweds would have to carry the basket together, signifying their partnership.

The creel was filled with stones and the groom was expected to carry it around the entire town. If he managed to do so without dropping it, the bride would join him and help him carry the creel for the rest of the journey. This was seen as a test of the groom's strength and the bride's willingness to share the burdens of life. The tradition was often accompanied by music, dancing, and a festive atmosphere. It was also a way for the community to participate in the celebration and to wish the couple well in their new life together.

- *Good fit for: Reception, Honeymoon*
- *Children or extended family participation: Not suitable/couple only*
- *Complexity: Easy*

Recommended Additional Reading:
"Irish Paganism: Unlocking Pagan Practices and Druidry in Ireland along with Welsh Witchcraft and Celtic Spirituality" by Mari Silva

"Pagan Ireland: Ritual and Belief in Another World" by John Waddell

CHAPTER 3 NORDIC AND VIKING HANDFASTING TRADITIONS

A Viking Romance

Long ago, in a remote Viking village nestled between towering fjords and icy waters, lived two young lovers, Astrid and Erik. Their love was as fierce as the storms that battered their homeland, and they longed to unite their souls in a Viking handfasting ceremony—an ancient engagement tradition passed down through generations.

Astrid was known for her fiery red hair and her spirit as untamed as the sea. She was a skilled shieldmaiden who could wield an axe with the strength of the mighty Thor himself. Erik, on the other hand, was a sturdy and steadfast warrior, respected by his fellow Vikings for his wisdom and courage.

As the snow-covered village prepared for the impending handfasting ceremony, the villagers gathered to help with the preparations. The longhouse was adorned with fur pelts, dragon-headed ships, and flickering torches, casting a warm glow upon the assembled guests. The village shaman, an old and wise woman named Freydis, prepared the sacred binding cords adorned with runes.

The day of the handfasting arrived with a crisp chill in the air. Astrid, dressed in a gown sewn with intricate Viking designs, her hair braided with wildflowers, stood at the entrance of the longhouse. Erik, in his best bear-skin cloak and with a sprig of mistletoe in his hand, approached her with a gleam in his eye.

The ceremony began with a haunting Viking chant led by Freydis, invoking the blessings of the gods. The couple stepped forward, hands clasped together, and Freydis draped the sacred cords over their wrists. She spoke words of wisdom and love, her voice carrying the weight of ages. With a single motion, she bound their hands together, creating a knot, which symbolized their commitment to each other during their engagement. The guests, all rugged and battle-hardened Vikings, watched in silence, their eyes filled with awe and reverence for the couple. As the sacred binding was completed, Astrid and Erik exchanged vows, promising to stand by each other's side through the fiercest storms and the darkest nights, as they embarked on their journey towards marriage.

With the ceremony concluded, the villagers erupted into cheers and applause, celebrating the beginning of a new chapter in the lives of Astrid and Erik. The feast that followed was nothing short of legendary, with tables laden with roast boar, mead flowing like a mighty river, and songs of valor and love echoing throughout the longhouse. As the night wore on, Astrid and Erik stole away from the revelry, hand in hand. They stood on the edge of the fjord, the Northern Lights dancing in the sky above them. In that moment, surrounded by the beauty of their homeland and the love of their people, they knew their handfasting had marked the start of a lifetime of adventures together.

And so, under the watchful eyes of the gods and the ancient traditions of their Viking ancestors, Astrid and Erik embarked on their engagement journey, knowing their love was as unbreakable as the bonds forged on that unforgettable day. As the tale of Astrid and Erik's Viking handfasting engagement ceremony spread throughout the land, it served as a reminder of the enduring power of love and the rich traditions which bound their Viking heritage together.

Nordic Versus Viking Handfastings

The main difference between Viking and Nordic handfasting lies in their historical specificity, cultural variations, and flexibility. Viking handfasting is more closely tied to the Viking Age and its specific customs, while Nordic handfasting encompasses a broader range of traditions from across the Nordic region and various historical periods. Couples may choose one or the other based on their historical interests and the degree of personalization they desire for their wedding ceremony.

The Viking Age roughly spans from the late 8th century to the early 11th century and is associated with the seafaring Norse people who originated in what is now modern-day Norway, Sweden, and Denmark. Viking handfasting ceremonies primarily pertain to this specific historical era.

Viking handfasting is rooted in the traditions of the Viking Age, which often involved ceremonies conducted within the context of Norse mythology and the worship of Norse gods.

"Nordic" is a broader term encompassing the cultures and traditions of the Scandinavian countries, including Denmark, Norway, Sweden, Finland, Iceland, and the Faroe Islands. Nordic handfasting may include practices from various historical periods and regions within this broader geographical context. Nordic handfasting ceremonies can be more flexible and adaptable.

Viking Rituals

A Viking handfasting ceremony would take place in a meaningful location, often outdoors in nature, such as near a forest, a river, or under the open sky. The choice of location held spiritual significance. The couple and their families would prepare for the event by gathering the necessary materials and adornments, which might include a decorated cloth or tapestry for the binding, flowers, and symbolic objects.

The bride and groom might inscribe runes on their clothing or ceremonial items to invoke blessings and protection. Brides often wore a crown made of metal or precious materials, such as silver or gold. These crowns were adorned with intricate designs, runes, or symbols representing fertility, protection, and prosperity. Some brides would carry a small axe during the ceremony, which symbolized her readiness to contribute to the household and protect her family.

Following the ceremony, a grand feast would be held in honor of the newly betrothed or married couple. The feast was a time for merriment, storytelling, and celebration. Food, drink, and music played an essential role in Viking celebrations, with mead and ale flowing freely, and songs and poems recounting heroic deeds and love stories. Norse runes, which held mystical significance, were often incorporated into wedding ceremonies.

1. Invocation of Deities:

The Viking handfasting ceremony began with an invocation to the Norse gods, such as Odin, Thor, Freyja, or Frigg. A local shaman or spiritual leader might perform this ritual, seeking the blessings of the gods for the couple's union. Viking weddings often included offerings to the spirits of deceased ancestors (Blót). These offerings were made to seek their guidance and blessings for the newlyweds.

- *Good fit for: engagement party, handfasting ceremony, house blessing*
- *Children or extended family participation: Suitable*
- *Complexity: Easy to Medium*

2. Exchange of Vows on Platform or Under Oak

The oak tree held significant symbolism for the Vikings and was considered sacred in Norse mythology and culture. The oak tree was associated with the chief god, Odin, who was considered the father of the gods and the ruler of Asgard. The oak tree represented his wisdom and his connection to the natural world. The word "oak" itself may have been derived from the Old Norse word "eik," which was associated with Odin. In Norse mythology, Yggdrasil was the World Tree, an enormous oak tree, which connected the nine worlds of Norse cosmology. It served as a central axis of the universe and represented the interconnectedness of all things in the cosmos. The Yggdrasil was seen as a representation of the cyclical nature of life, death, and rebirth.

In some regions, the ritual was performed beneath an oak tree. The couple would stand together, often on a raised platform or a mound, to exchange their vows. The couple would exchange vows and tokens under the tree's branches, seeking the blessings of the gods. The gothi (officiant) would invoke the gods and goddesses, asking for their blessings and protection over the couple. The couple would then exchange rings, a symbol of their eternal bond and commitment to each other. The rings were often made of gold or silver and were sometimes inscribed with runes or symbols of the gods.

- *Good fit for: engagement ceremony, handfasting ceremony*
- *Children or extended family participation: Not suitable*
- *Complexity: Easy*

3. Exchange of Tokens - Sword and Shield

To seal their commitment, the couple might exchange tokens or gifts. These could be symbolic items, such as rings, keys, or symbolic tools representing their roles in the partnership. These gifts could include valuable items like jewelry, weapons, or tools and symbolized the couple's wealth and status. In some Viking weddings, the groom would offer his bride a sword as a symbol of his commitment and protection. The bride, in turn, might offer her groom a shield, signifying her support and defense of their home. In other cases, the couple might exchange personal items, such as pieces of clothing or jewelry holding sentimental value. These items were often passed down through generations, symbolizing the couple's connection to their ancestors and their commitment to continue their family's legacy.

The exchange of gifts was not limited to the couple. The families of the bride and groom also exchanged gifts as a sign of their mutual respect and acceptance of the union. These gifts could be anything from livestock to land, depending on the wealth and status of the families involved. The exchange of gifts was a significant part of the Viking wedding ceremony, symbolizing the couple's commitment to each other and their new roles as husband and wife. Gifts were also a way for the couple to publicly display their wealth and status, as well as their connection to their families and ancestors.

- *Good fit for: handfasting ceremony, reception, honeymoon*
- *Children or extended family participation: Not suitable*
- *Complexity: Easy*

4. Fire and Smoke

Fire was an essential element in Viking weddings. The couple would often leap over a fire or pass through its smoke as a purification and protection ritual. The fire was believed to ward off evil spirits. The fire was also used to light the wedding feast, which was a significant part of the Viking wedding ceremony. The feast was a grand affair, often lasting for several days, and was attended by the couple's families, friends, and the entire community. The fire was also symbolic of the couple's new life together. As the fire was lit from a spark, the couple's love was expected to grow and flourish. The fire was kept burning throughout the wedding ceremony and the subsequent feast, symbolizing the couple's enduring love and commitment to each other. It was a testament to the Vikings' deep respect for the natural elements and their belief in their spiritual power. Keep safety in mind, including the capability of the couple, when including fire rituals such as this.

- *Good fit for: engagement ceremony, handfasting ceremony, reception, honeymoon*
- *Children or extended family participation: Not suitable*
- *Complexity: Medium-Advanced (safety precautions needed for working with fire and see chapter on Risk Management and Other Considerations)*

5. Bread and Salt

A Viking bride and groom would break a loaf of bread over each other's heads, symbolizing the sharing of food and the promise to care for one another's needs. Salt was then sprinkled on the broken bread as a symbol of purification. This tradition was a significant part of the Viking wedding ceremony, known as the "Bridal-Quest." The breaking of bread was a public declaration of the couple's commitment to each other. It was a promise that they would provide for each other's needs, both physical and emotional.

The bread used in this ceremony was often a special loaf, baked specifically for the occasion. It was a hearty, dense bread, symbolizing the strength and resilience of the marriage. The act of breaking the bread was not a gentle one; it was done with force, symbolizing the challenges that the couple would face together in their married life. The sprinkling of salt on the broken bread was a symbol of purification and protection. Salt was considered a powerful substance in Viking culture, capable of warding off evil spirits. By sprinkling salt on the bread, the couple was invoking protection for their marriage. This tradition was not only a symbolic act; it was also a practical one. The broken pieces of bread were often shared with the wedding guests, symbolizing the couple's willingness to share their resources with their community. This act of generosity was seen as a good omen for the couple's future prosperity.

- *Good fit for: engagement ceremony, handfasting ceremony*
- *Children or extended family participation: Not suitable*
- *Complexity: Easy*

Nordic Rituals

Nordic handfasting celebrations overlap in many of the rituals described above under Viking rituals. Here are a few that differ.

1. Midsummer Celebrations

Nordic handfasting ceremonies often incorporate elements of Midsummer celebrations, which are a significant tradition in Nordic countries. These may include dancing around a maypole, lighting bonfires, and celebrating the longest day of the year. The couple may exchange vows or perform rituals during the height of the Midsummer festivities. The ceremony is often held outdoors, in a forest or by a body of water, to honor the natural world and the spirits, which inhabit it. The couple may also make offerings to the gods and goddesses of the Nordic pantheon, asking for their blessings and protection.

In Nordic countries, especially Sweden, a central feature of Midsummer is the raising of a Maypole (or Midsummer Pole), which is decorated with greenery and flowers. You could include a smaller version of a Maypole at your ceremony. The couple and wedding party participants could weave ribbons around the pole as part of their handfasting ritual, symbolizing the intertwining of their lives. This could be incorporated into a contemporary handfasting ceremony or reception.

During the Midsummer celebrations, the couple may participate in traditional dances and games. They may also light a bonfire, which is believed to ward off evil spirits and bring good luck. The bonfire is often kept burning throughout the night, symbolizing the couple's enduring love and commitment to each other. The Midsummer feast is another important part of the celebration. The couple and their guests may enjoy traditional Nordic dishes, such as pickled herring, smoked salmon, and fresh berries. They may also drink mead, a honey-based alcoholic beverage popular in ancient Nordic societies. The bonfire and feast traditions could be included in a modern handfasting reception celebration.

- *Good fit for: proposal, engagement ceremony, party or dinner, bachelorette party, bachelor party, handfasting ceremony, reception, honeymoon*
- *Children or extended family participation: Suitable*
- *Complexity: Easy-Medium*

2. Samhain or Winter Solstice Rituals

Some Nordic handfasting ceremonies are timed to coincide with Samhain (the festival marking the end of the harvest season) or the Winter Solstice (the shortest day of the year). These ceremonies may include rituals related to honoring the changing seasons, ancestral spirits, or the transition from darkness to light. During a Samhain handfasting ceremony, the couple may honor the end of the harvest season by incorporating elements such as grains, fruits, and vegetables into the ceremony. They may also pay tribute to their ancestors by setting up an altar with photos and mementos of their loved ones. The ceremony may also include a ritual to ward off evil spirits, such as carving protective symbols into a pumpkin or lighting a bonfire.

A Winter Solstice handfasting ceremony, on the other hand, may focus on the theme of transition from darkness to light. The couple may light a Yule log together, symbolizing the return of the sun and the promise of longer days ahead. They may also exchange vows during the moment of the solstice, when the day is shortest and the night is longest, to symbolize their commitment to each other through both the dark and light times in their lives. In both ceremonies, the couple's hands are bound together with a cord or ribbon while they recite their vows. This act symbolizes their commitment to each other and their intention to stay together through all the seasons of life. After the ceremony, the couple may keep the cord as a reminder of their vows and the special day when they became one.

- *Good fit for: proposal, engagement ceremony, party or dinner, bachelorette party, bachelor party, handfasting ceremony, reception, honeymoon*
- *Children or extended family participation: Suitable*
- *Complexity: Easy-Medium*

3. *Huldufólk or Hidden Folk Honoring*

In Icelandic tradition, there's a belief in the huldufólk, or hidden folk, who are considered to be the elves, fairies and hidden spirits of the land. Some Nordic ceremonies incorporate rituals or offerings to honor these beings as part of the celebration. The huldufólk are believed to live in a parallel world in the rocks, hills, and mountains of Iceland. They are often described as being similar in appearance to humans, but with some key differences such as being smaller in size, and often wearing old-fashioned Icelandic clothing. They are also believed to have the ability to make themselves invisible at will. The belief in huldufólk is ingrained in Icelandic culture.

During certain ceremonies, such as at Midsummer, New Year's Eve, and Yule, it is traditional to leave out food and drink for the huldufólk. This is done as a sign of respect and to ensure good luck for the coming year. Some people also believe: if you treat the huldufólk well, they will help you in return, while if you disrespect them, they will cause misfortune. In addition to these offerings, there are also rituals performed to honor the huldufólk. These can include dances, songs, and stories told about them. These rituals are often performed in places believed to be inhabited by the huldufólk, such as in the countryside or near certain rocks and hills. Despite the modernization of Iceland, the belief in huldufólk and the traditions associated with them continue to be a significant part of Icelandic culture. They serve as a reminder of the country's rich folklore and the deep respect that Icelanders have for nature and the unseen world.

The huldufólk, or hidden folk, are rooted in Icelandic folklore and cultural identity, but they are not typically a central part of Icelandic handfasting traditions or modern wedding ceremonies. However, the respect for nature and the mystical which is embodied in the lore of the huldufólk might indirectly influence the ambiance or theme of an Icelandic handfasting ceremony. For instance, choosing a ceremony location honoring the beauty and sanctity of nature could be seen as aligning with the spirit of the huldufólk traditions. Additionally, couples who have a deep personal connection to Icelandic folklore might choose to include references to these tales in their ceremony as a nod to their cultural heritage.

- *Good fit for: proposal, engagement ceremony, party or dinner, handfasting ceremony, reception, home blessing*
- *Children or extended family participation: Suitable*
- *Complexity: Easy-Medium*

4. Tree Planting

Nordic handfasting ceremonies often emphasize a strong connection to nature. In a Nordic handfasting ceremony, the couple may choose to plant a tree together. This ritual symbolizes the growth of their relationship, their commitment to nurturing each other, and their connection to the earth. The tree is often chosen for its symbolic meaning. For example, an oak tree might be chosen for its strength and longevity, while a fruit tree might symbolize fertility and abundance.

- *Good fit for: engagement ceremony, party or dinner, handfasting ceremony, reception, honeymoon*
- *Children or extended family participation: Suitable*
- *Complexity: Easy*

5. Love Lock

Couples make or creating a "love lock" and attach it to a natural feature like a bridge or a tree to symbolize their commitment to each other and the environment. A love lock is a padlock that they lock onto a bridge or a tree and then throw away the key, symbolizing their unbreakable bond. This tradition is believed to have originated from a Serbian tale during World War I, where a woman died of heartbreak when her lover went to war and fell in love with another woman. The women in the town, wanting to protect their own love stories, started writing their names and the names of their loved ones on padlocks and affixing them to the bridge where the woman used to meet her lover.

Today, love locks can be found on bridges, fences, gates, and trees around the world. Some of the most famous love lock locations include the Pont des Arts in Paris, the Hohenzollern Bridge in Cologne, and the N Seoul Tower in South Korea. Creating a love lock can be a romantic and meaningful activity for couples. They can purchase a padlock and write or engrave their names on it. Some couples also include a special date or a short message. Once the lock is secured, they throw away the key, symbolizing their everlasting love and commitment to each other.

While this tradition is romantic, it can also be harmful to the environment and the structures where the locks are placed. The weight of numerous locks can damage bridges and other structures, and keys thrown into rivers can pollute the water. Some cities have started removing love locks to protect their landmarks. Therefore, if you're considering creating a love lock, it's important to think about the potential impact on the environment and local landmarks.

Consider alternatives like virtual love locks, or choose locations where love locks are allowed and managed in a way that minimizes harm. Or create one on an object you can display at your own home.

- *Good fit for: proposal, engagement ceremony, reception, honeymoon*
- *Children or extended family participation: Suitable*
- *Complexity: Easy*

Recommended Additional Reading:
"The Viking Hondbók: Eat, Dress, and Fight Like a Warrior" by Kjersti Egerdahl

"Pagan Magic of the Northern Tradition: Customs, Rites, and Ceremonies" by Nigel Pennick

"Norse Paganism for Beginners: An Essential Guide to the Norse Pagan Religion, Gods, Goddesses, Asatru, Viking Rituals, Nordic Magic, Runes, and Spells (Scandinavian Spirituality)" by Silvia Hill

CHAPTER 4 SLAVIC HANDFASTING TRADITIONS

Slavic Saga of Love

Years ago, in a quaint Slavic village nestled deep within the lush forests and rolling hills of Eastern Europe, there lived two young lovers, Milena and Ivan. Their love was as enduring as the changing seasons, and they longed to unite their souls in a traditional Slavic handfasting ceremony, a celebration rooted in their ancestral heritage.

In the heart of the village, the entire community came together to prepare for Milena and Ivan's handfasting. The couple's families and neighbors gathered at the village square, where a grand feast was laid out under a colorful canopy. Tables groaned under the weight of dishes filled with pierogi, sauerkraut, roast meats, and freshly baked bread. The aroma of honey cakes and sweet fruit wine filled the air.

As the sun dipped below the horizon, the villagers lit a bonfire at the center of the square. The flames flickered and danced, casting a warm glow over the gathering. A village elder, Zofia, stepped forward, holding a beautifully embroidered cloth. Zofia placed the embroidered cloth over Milena and Ivan, symbolizing their unity. As they stood beneath the veil, their souls intertwined, they pledged their love and devotion to each other. It was a moment of pure connection, surrounded by the support and love of their community.

Milena gifted Ivan a carved wooden pendant of Perun, the god of thunder, signifying protection and strength. In return, Ivan offered Milena a delicate silver necklace adorned with the symbol of Mokosh, the goddess of fertility, representing prosperity and abundance. A large round loaf of bread, called kolach, was brought forward. The couple took a piece of bread and dipped it in salt, symbolizing the blessings of life and the challenges they would face together. They fed each other the bread, signifying their commitment to nourish and care for one another.

With the ceremonial rituals complete, the villagers formed a circle around the bonfire, hand in hand. A fiddler played a lively tune, and the villagers began to dance. Milena and Ivan, their hands still bound beneath the embroidered cloth, joined the circle dance, moving to the music's rhythm. As they danced, they felt the energy of the community and the spirits of their ancestors surrounding them.

As the night wore on, the time came to unbind Milena and Ivan. Zofia carefully removed the embroidered cloth from their shoulders, signifying the end of the ceremony. The couple, now officially joined in love, kissed beneath the starry sky, and the villagers erupted into cheers and applause.

The celebration continued long into the night, with laughter, music, and the sharing of stories and wisdom. Under the light of the bonfire, Milena and Ivan's love was sealed, not only in the eyes of their community but also in the cherished traditions of their Slavic ancestors.

Slavic Handfasting Rituals

Slavic culture encompasses a group of countries and regions in Eastern and Central Europe where Slavic languages, traditions, and heritage are prevalent. Slavic Paganism, also known as Rodnovery or Rodnoveryje, is a polytheistic and nature-based religious belief system, which was practiced by the early Slavic peoples of Eastern Europe before the widespread Christianization of the region. It is rooted in the spiritual traditions and folklore of the Slavic-speaking communities and is characterized by a reverence for nature, ancestor worship, and a pantheon of gods and spirits.

Slavic Paganism places a strong emphasis on honoring and communicating with ancestors. Ancestral spirits are seen as protectors and guides, and rituals are performed to maintain a connection with the deceased. Nature plays a central role in Slavic Paganism. The natural world, including forests, rivers, and mountains, is considered sacred. Many Slavic rituals and festivals are tied to the changing seasons and natural cycles. Slavic Pagans often practiced divination and magic, using methods such as reading signs in nature, dream interpretation, and the use of herbs and charms for protection and healing.

Explore a myriad of Slavic handfasting traditions, each unique and steeped in rich cultural heritage, originating from diverse regions across Eastern Europe:

Bulgaria

1. Stepping on Eggs
The bride's family gathers a number of eggs and decorates them. These eggs are hard-boiled and may be painted or adorned with colorful designs. During the handfasting ceremony, as the couple stands at the entrance of their new home or at the church entrance, they are presented with a tray of decorated eggs. The eggs may be arranged in a decorative pattern. The bride and groom take turns stepping on the eggs, attempting to crush them with their heels. The goal is to see who can break more eggs. It's a playful and lighthearted competition.

Eggs symbolize fertility and new beginnings. The act of breaking the egg, which releases something new, aligns with the couple embarking on a new life together. The ritual symbolizes the couple's ability to work together and support each other in their marriage. It also represents their hopes for a fertile and prosperous life together. The eggs, which are fragile, signify the challenges they may face and their ability to overcome them as a team.

- *Good fit for: engagement ceremony, party or dinner, handfasting ceremony, reception, honeymoon*
- *Children or extended family participation: Suitable*
- *Complexity: Easy*

2. Stepping on Wheat

Before the handfasting ceremony, a plate filled with wheat kernels or rice grains is prepared. Sometimes, the wheat or rice may be mixed with other symbolic items, such as coins or herbs. During the handfasting ceremony, as the couple stands together, they are presented with the plate of wheat or rice. The plate is often placed at the entrance of the church or the couple's new home. The bride and groom take turns stepping on the plate of wheat or rice, attempting to crush the grains with their heels. The goal is to see who can break more grains. Like the "stepping on eggs" tradition, it's a playful and lighthearted competition. As they exchange vows, they also step on the plate, symbolizing fertility and abundance in their life together. After the ceremony, the broken pieces of the plate are collected and kept as a symbol of good luck.

This tradition is believed to bring prosperity and happiness to the newlyweds. The act of stepping on the plate also signifies the couple's ability to overcome obstacles together. The wheat or rice in the plate represents the hope for a fruitful and prosperous life. It is also a symbol of fertility, wishing the couple a family filled with children.

- *Good fit for: engagement ceremony, party or dinner, bridal shower, bachelor party, reception, honeymoon, house blessing*
- *Children or extended family participation: Suitable*
- *Complexity: Easy*

3. Bridal Circle Dance (Horo)

The horo is a traditional Bulgarian dance performed in a circle. The bride and groom are often invited to lead the horo, which symbolizes their unity and the circle of life. Guests join hands and dance together, celebrating the couple's joy. The horo dance may be accompanied by traditional Bulgarian music, often played on instruments such as the gaida (a type of bagpipe), gadulka (a string instrument), and tapan (a large drum). The dance steps are often simple, allowing everyone to participate, regardless of their dancing skills.

The horo can vary in complexity, from simple walking steps to intricate footwork, depending on the region of Bulgaria it originates from. Some versions of the horo involve dancers moving in a line or semi-circle, rather than a full circle. The horo is more than a dance; it is a social event bringing the community together. It is a symbol of Bulgarian culture and tradition, often performed at weddings, festivals, and other celebrations.

- *Good fit for: engagement ceremony or party, reception*
- *Children or extended family participation: Suitable*
- *Complexity: Easy*

Bosnia

1. Cup of Wine

In some Bosnian Slavic handfastings, the couple shares a cup of wine. The wine represents the sweetness and richness of life, and by sharing it, they signify their intention to share all aspects of their future life together. This tradition is a symbolic gesture signifying unity, love, and commitment. The couple takes turns to drink from the same cup, symbolizing their willingness to share everything in their life, both the joys and the sorrows. This ritual is often performed during the handfasting ceremony after the exchange of vows and rings.

The wine used in this ritual is often sweet, symbolizing the sweetness of love and the richness of a life shared together. It is also a symbol of fertility and prosperity, wishing the couple a fruitful and prosperous marriage. In some variations of this tradition, the couple may also share a piece of bread, symbolizing their commitment to provide for each other, and salt, symbolizing the preservation of their union.

- *Good fit for: proposal, engagement ceremony, party or dinner, bachelorette party, bachelor party, rehearsal dinner, handfasting ceremony, reception, honeymoon*
- *Children or extended family participation: Not Suitable*
- *Complexity: Easy*

2. Henna Night

The bride may have a henna night, or "nights of the henna" (noći koja), before the handfasting ceremony. Henna is applied to her hands and feet in intricate designs. It is believed to bring good luck and protect the bride from evil spirits. The henna night is a traditional pre-wedding ceremony, popular in many cultures, particularly in the Middle East, North Africa, and South Asia. The bride's female friends and family members gather to celebrate and participate in the application of henna. The designs are often floral and geometric patterns and can take several hours to apply. The henna paste is made from the leaves of the henna plant, which are dried and ground into a fine powder. This powder is mixed with water, lemon juice, and essential oils to create a paste. The paste is then applied to the skin using a small cone or brush. After the henna is applied, it is left to dry for several hours or overnight. The dried henna is then scraped off, leaving a reddish-brown stain on the skin that can last for up to two weeks.

The henna night is about more than beautifying the bride. It is also a time for the bride to relax and enjoy the company of her loved ones before the wedding. It is a time for laughter, storytelling, and bonding. The henna night is a cherished tradition adding a touch of cultural heritage and symbolism to the handfasting festivities.

- *Good fit for: rehearsal dinner, preparation for handfasting ceremony*
- *Children or extended family participation: Not Suitable*
- *Complexity: Medium to Advanced*

3. Bosnian Coffee Ritual

Bosnian coffee, a strong and finely ground coffee prepared using a special pot called a "džezva," is an essential part of Bosnian culture. At the handfasting, the bride serves coffee to the groom and his family as a symbol of her hospitality and readiness to become a part of their family. The process of making Bosnian coffee is a ritual in itself. The coffee beans are first roasted and then ground into a very fine powder. The coffee is then brewed in the džezva, a small copper or brass pot with a long handle. The dževza is filled with water and the coffee is added. The mixture is then brought to a boil over a low heat. Once the coffee has boiled, it is removed from the heat and allowed to settle before being poured into small, handle-less cups called "fildžan." The coffee is served with a cube of sugar or a piece of Turkish delight on the side. The sugar or candy is placed in the mouth before drinking the coffee, creating a unique blend of sweet and bitter flavors.

The tradition of the bride serving coffee at the wedding is a significant one. It is a way for the bride to show her respect and willingness to serve her new family. It is also a way for the groom's family to judge the bride's character and skills. If the coffee is well-prepared, it is a sign the bride is capable and ready to take on the responsibilities of being a wife and mother. In Bosnian culture, coffee is more than a mere beverage. It is a symbol of hospitality, respect, and community. Whether it's a daily ritual or a special occasion like a wedding, Bosnian coffee is a cherished tradition that brings people together.

- *Good fit for: handfasting ceremony or reception*
- *Children or extended family participation: Suitable*
- *Complexity: Medium*

4. Bridge Crossing

A playful Bosnian tradition involves the groom and his party arriving at the bride's home and requesting permission to cross a "bridge" (a scarf or a piece of cloth), which the bride's family holds. This ritual may include symbolic negotiations and humor. The groom and his party may offer gifts or money to the bride's family in exchange for permission to cross the bridge. The bride's family may also playfully refuse the groom's request several times before finally allowing him to cross. This tradition is a fun and lighthearted way to symbolize the joining of two families.

- *Good fit for: engagement ceremony, party or dinner, house blessing*

- *Children or extended family participation: Suitable*
- *Complexity: Easy*

<u>Croatia</u>

1. Release of Doves

In Croatian Slavic weddings, it's common for the newlyweds to release a pair of doves. This act symbolizes love, peace, and the beginning of their new life together. Doves are seen as messengers of happiness and harmony. In addition to this, the flight of the doves is believed to predict the couple's future. If the doves fly together, it is seen as a sign of a harmonious and happy marriage. If they fly in different directions, it is interpreted as a sign of potential challenges or disagreements in the future. However, regardless of the direction the doves take, their release is always a beautiful and meaningful moment in Croatian weddings.

The tradition of releasing doves is not exclusive to Croatia but is also practiced in other cultures around the world. It is a universal symbol of love, peace, and unity, making it a fitting ritual for a wedding ceremony.

In addition to the dove release, Croatian weddings are also known for their lively music, traditional dances, and delicious food. The celebration often lasts for several days, with the entire community coming together to celebrate the union of the newlyweds. Note it is important to hire a reputable, sustainable handler with references when introducing live animals into a ritual.

- *Good fit for: handfasting ceremony, reception*
- *Children or extended family participation: Not Suitable*

- *Complexity: Advanced*

2. Invocation of Nature Spirits

Croatian Pagan couples may choose to invoke the spirits of nature, such as the guardian spirits of the forest, the river, or the land. These invocations can be done through songs, prayers, or recitations. The couple may also choose to perform rituals involving offerings to these spirits. These offerings can be in the form of food, drink, or other items considered valuable or sacred. For example, they might offer fruits and vegetables from their own garden, homemade bread or wine, or handcrafted items.

The rituals can take place in a variety of settings, depending on the spirits being invoked. For instance, a ritual to honor the spirits of the forest might take place in a wooded area, while a ritual for the spirits of the river might be performed near a body of water. During these rituals, the couple may also recite vows or make promises to each other. These vows can be traditional or personalized, and they often reflect the couple's commitment to each other and to the natural world.

- *Good fit for: engagement ceremony, party or dinner, bridal shower, bachelor party, handfasting ceremony, reception, honeymoon, house blessing*
- *Children or extended family participation: Suitable*
- *Complexity: Medium*

Czech Republic

1. Rosemary Crowns

In the Czech Republic, it's a tradition to weave crowns or wreaths made of rosemary branches and flowers for the bride and groom. These crowns symbolize love, fidelity, and happiness. The couple is crowned during the ceremony, and the crowns are often exchanged between them.

The tradition of weaving crowns from rosemary branches and flowers is rooted in Czech culture. Rosemary is a symbol of love and fidelity, and it is believed to bring happiness and good luck to the newlyweds. The crowns may be made by the bride's family or friends, and they are often decorated with other flowers, ribbons, and beads. The crowning ceremony is a significant part of the wedding. The bride and groom stand before the officiant, who places the crowns on their heads. The crowns are then exchanged between the couple, symbolizing their unity and shared responsibilities in their new life together. After the wedding, the crowns are often kept as a memento of the special day. Some couples choose to hang them in their home as a reminder of their vows and the love they share. This tradition is not unique to the Czech Republic but is also found in other Slavic cultures. It is a beautiful and meaningful way to celebrate the union of two people in love.

- *Good fit for: engagement party, bridal shower, handfasting ceremony*
- *Children or extended family participation: Suitable*
- *Complexity: Medium – Advanced*

2. Herb and Flower Blessing

As part of the ceremony, Czech Republic Pagan couples exchange or sprinkle each other with herbs and flowers having symbolic meanings, such as lavender for love, rosemary for fidelity, and chamomile for prosperity. This tradition is rooted in the Pagan belief system, which places a strong emphasis on the power of nature and its elements.

The herbs and flowers used in the ceremony are chosen for their symbolic meanings as well as for their magical properties. Lavender, for instance, is believed to attract love and promote peace and tranquility. Rosemary, on the other hand, is associated with remembrance and fidelity, making it a fitting symbol for a marriage ceremony. Chamomile, with its bright, cheerful flowers, is believed to bring prosperity and good luck.

The exchange or sprinkling of these herbs and flowers is a way for the couple to express their commitment to each other and their hopes for their future together. It is also a way for them to connect with the natural world and the forces, which they believe govern their lives. The ceremony is conducted by a Pagan priest or priestess, who guides the couple through the ritual and blesses their union.

- *Good fit for: engagement ceremony, party or dinner, handfasting ceremony, reception, house blessing*
- *Children or extended family participation: Suitable*
- *Complexity: Easy-Medium*

Macedonia (Southeastern region of the Balkan Peninsula)

1. Bread and Salt Home Welcome
In Macedonian Slavic handfastings, the bride's family welcomes the groom and his party with bread and salt at the entrance of the bride's home. The groom must take a bite of bread and a pinch of salt to show his willingness to be part

of the family. This tradition is a symbolic gesture of hospitality and acceptance. The bread represents the family's willingness to provide for the groom, while the salt symbolizes the hardships they are willing to endure together. The groom's acceptance of the bread and salt signifies his commitment to join the family and share in both their joys and struggles.

- *Good fit for: engagement dinner, house blessing*
- *Children or extended family participation: Suitable*
- *Complexity: Easy*

2. Circle Dance (Oro)

A traditional Macedonian circle dance, known as the "oro," is part of the event. The circle represents unity, continuity, and the cyclical nature of life. Invite your handfasting guests to join in the dance to celebrate your love. The oro is a beautiful and symbolic tradition. As everyone join hands and forms a circle, they are reminded of the unity and continuity that love brings. The circle, unbroken and unending, represents the eternal nature of the group's love for each other. As they dance, they move in rhythm with the music, their steps echoing the beat of their hearts. This dance is a celebration of love and life.

- *Good fit for: engagement party or dinner, reception*
- *Children or extended family participation: Suitable*
- *Complexity: Easy*

Poland

1. Bridal Dance with Gifts

In the Silesian region of Poland, the bride dances with her guests while holding a basket. As she dances, guests place money and gifts in the basket. This tradition symbolizes well-wishes for the couple's future and helps with their financial start as a married couple. This tradition is not only a fun and interactive part of the wedding celebration, but it also serves a practical purpose. The money and gifts collected can be used by the newlyweds to set up their new home, pay for their honeymoon, or cover other expenses related to their new life together. The dance takes place during the wedding reception, after the formalities of the ceremony are over. The bride, dressed in her wedding gown, carries a decorated basket and dances with each guest in turn. The guests, in return for the dance, place their gifts or money in the basket.

This tradition is a way for the community to show their support and love for the newlyweds. It is also a way for the bride to personally thank each guest for their presence and their gift. The dance is often accompanied by traditional Silesian music, adding to the festive atmosphere of the occasion. The amount of money or the value of the gift is not as important as the act of giving itself. It is a gesture of goodwill, a wish for the couple's happiness and prosperity. The bride's dance with the guests is a joyful and meaningful part of a Silesian wedding, a tradition which strengthens the bonds between the couple and their community.

- *Good fit for: engagement party, reception*
- *Children or extended family participation: Suitable*
- *Complexity: Easy*

2. Throwing Grains

During the reception, the bride and groom may throw grains, such as wheat or rice, over each other's heads. This symbolizes fertility and abundance in their married life. This tradition is common in many cultures around the world. The act of throwing grains is believed to bring prosperity, fertility, and good luck to the newlyweds.

In some cultures, guests also participate in this tradition by throwing grains at the couple as they exit the ceremony or reception. This is often seen as a fun and festive way to celebrate the couple's new life together. In addition to symbolizing fertility and abundance, the grains can also represent the couple's hopes and dreams for their future together. Each grain can symbolize a different wish or blessing, such as happiness, health, wealth, or longevity.

While this tradition is often associated with weddings, it can also be incorporated into other celebrations or ceremonies. For example, it can be used in housewarming parties to wish the homeowners abundance and prosperity in their new home. Regardless of the occasion, the act of throwing grains is a beautiful and meaningful tradition adding a touch of symbolism and sentimentality to any celebration. Take care to choose environmentally friendly grains or substitute lavender buds. Check with the venue in advance to ensure it is allowed.

- *Good fit for: reception*
- *Children or extended family participation: Suitable*
- *Complexity: Easy-Medium*

3. Wreath Exchange

In some regions of Poland, it's customary for the bride and groom to exchange floral wreaths. The wreaths are placed on each other's heads to symbolize their union and the beginning of their life together. This tradition is rooted in Polish culture and history. The wreaths may be made of myrtle or rosemary, which symbolize love, fidelity, and remembrance. They are often decorated with ribbons and other adornments in the wedding colors. The exchange of wreaths is a significant moment in the wedding ceremony.

The bride and groom each take their wreath and place it on the other's head, often with the help of the best man and maid of honor. This act is accompanied by a blessing from the priest or officiant, who may also sprinkle the couple with holy water. The wreaths are worn throughout the wedding ceremony and reception, serving as a visible symbol of the couple's commitment to each other. They are often kept as a memento after the wedding, serving as a reminder of the special day. The direction in which the wreaths float is said to predict the direction in which the couple's life will take them.

- *Good fit for: handfasting ceremony, reception*
- *Children or extended family participation: Suitable*
- *Complexity: Easy*

<u>Russia</u>

1. The Breaking of Glass
In Russian Slavic handfastings, it is a tradition for the couple to jointly break a glass wrapped in a cloth. The breaking of the glass symbolizes the fragility of human relationships and serves as a reminder of the challenges and uncertainties that may lie ahead. The number of shards the glass breaks into is also considered significant. It is believed each piece represents a year of happy marriage. Therefore, the more

pieces the glass breaks into, the more years of happiness the couple is expected to have. The breaking of the glass is also a moment of transition, marking the end of the wedding ceremony and the beginning of the celebration. It is a moment of joy and celebration, as well as a moment of reflection and contemplation. It serves as a reminder that even in the happiest moments, one must remain aware of the challenges which life may bring.

Consider safety measures around broken glass.

- *Good fit for: handfasting ceremony, reception*
- *Children or extended family participation: Not Suitable*
- *Complexity: Easy-Medium*

2. Bread and Salt Reception Ceremony
In Russian Slavic handfastings, the couple is welcomed with bread and salt upon their arrival at the reception. The bread, often adorned with a decorative cloth, symbolizes prosperity, while the salt represents the essential element of life. The couple takes a bite of bread and a pinch of salt as a gesture of hospitality and the shared challenges of life. The couple's parents present the bread and salt. The couple then breaks off a piece of bread, dips it in the salt, and eats it.

This ritual is a symbol of the couple's commitment to care for each other and their future family. It also signifies their readiness to endure life's hardships together. The bread and salt tradition is not only limited to weddings. It is also a common custom in many Slavic countries to welcome guests, especially distinguished or honored ones, with bread and salt. This tradition is rooted in the Slavic culture and is considered a sign of friendship and hospitality.

In some variations of the tradition, the couple also drinks wine after eating the bread and salt. The wine symbolizes the sweetness and joys of life. The combination of bread, salt, and wine thus represents a balance of prosperity, hardship, and joy in the couple's life together. The bread and salt ritual is a beautiful and meaningful tradition adding a unique touch to Russian Slavic handfastings. It is a testament to the couple's commitment to each other and their readiness to face life's challenges together.

- *Good fit for: engagement dinner, reception*
- *Children or extended family participation: Suitable*
- *Complexity: Easy*

3. Wearing Bread on Shoulders
The tradition of wearing bread on the shoulders during a handfasting is a Slavic custom, particularly associated with countries in Eastern Europe. It is commonly practiced in countries like Ukraine, Russia, and Poland, among others. The bread is often a special type of bread known as "korovai" in Ukraine or "karavai" in Russia. This bread is elaborately decorated and holds symbolic significance in the handfasting ceremony, representing prosperity, fertility, and hospitality. The act of the newlyweds each taking a bite from the bread as it rests on their shoulders symbolizes their shared commitment to providing for each other in their married life. This tradition is a beautiful and meaningful part of many Slavic wedding ceremonies.

- *Good fit for: engagement ceremony, handfasting ceremony, reception*
- *Children or extended family participation: Not Suitable*
- *Complexity: Easy*

Serbia

1. Mock Kidnapping of the Bride
In some Serbian Slavic handfastings, friends and family playfully "kidnap" the bride before the handfasting ceremony. The groom must negotiate her release with gifts and gestures of love, showing his determination to win her heart. This tradition, known as "bride-napping," is a fun and playful part of the wedding festivities in some Serbian communities. It is a symbolic act representing the groom's commitment and willingness to do whatever it takes to be with his bride.

The kidnapping usually happens during the pre-wedding celebrations. The bride's friends and family members whisk her away to a secret location. The groom is then informed of the kidnapping and is tasked with finding his bride-to-be. The negotiation process is often filled with humor and good-natured teasing. The groom may be asked to perform tasks, answer riddles, or present gifts to the bride's family and friends. These tasks are designed to demonstrate his love, commitment, and suitability as a husband. Once the groom has successfully negotiated the bride's release, the handfasting ceremony can proceed. This tradition adds a unique and entertaining element to the wedding festivities, and it is a cherished part of Serbian Slavic culture.

- *Good fit for: engagement party or dinner, rehearsal dinner*

- *Children or extended family participation: Suitable*
- *Complexity: Easy-Medium*

2. Sharing Bitterness and Sweetness

In Serbian Slavic weddings, the couple tastes a spoonful of honey and a spoonful of red pepper paste. The sweetness of the honey symbolizes the joys of life, while the bitterness of the pepper paste represents the challenges. This ritual emphasizes the balance of experiences in marriage. The couple is reminded they will share both the sweet and bitter moments together, supporting each other through all the ups and downs. This tradition is a beautiful representation of the commitment and unity that marriage entails.

The couple is also often given bread, salt, and wine, which symbolize prosperity, longevity, and the spice of life, respectively. The Serbian wedding ceremony is rich in symbolism and tradition, reflecting the importance of marriage in Serbian culture. It is a celebration of love, commitment, and the joining of two families. The rituals performed during the ceremony are meant to bless the couple with a long, happy, and prosperous life together.

The honey and red pepper paste ritual is one of many unique traditions that make Serbian weddings so special. It is a beautiful reminder of the balance of life and the importance of sharing both the good and the bad times with your partner. It is a testament to the strength and resilience of the marital bond.

- *Good fit for: engagement dinner, handfasting ceremony, reception*
- *Children or extended family participation: Not Suitable*
- *Complexity: Easy*

3. Tying of Hands with Towel
While not a handfasting cord in the traditional sense, some Serbian couples may have their hands tied together with a special towel during the ceremony. This symbolizes their union and commitment. This practice is known as "vezivanje ruku" or "binding of hands". The towel used is often intricately decorated or embroidered, sometimes with the couple's initials or wedding date. The priest or officiant ties the couple's hands together, symbolizing their unity and the bond they are forming through marriage. This ritual is similar to the Celtic tradition of handfasting, where the couple's hands are tied together with a cord or ribbon. Both practices symbolize the couple's commitment to each other and their new life together.

- *Good fit for: engagement ceremony, handfasting ceremony*

- *Children or extended family participation: Suitable*
- *Complexity: Easy-Medium*

Slovakia

1. Ceremonial Broom Jump
In some Slovakian Slavic weddings, the couple is presented with a ceremonial broom. They must jump over it together, symbolizing the sweeping away of their old lives and the beginning of a clean, new chapter together. This tradition is a symbolic act representing the couple's commitment to work together in their new life. The broom is often decorated with flowers and ribbons, and the couple must jump over it without touching it. If they succeed, it is believed to bring good luck and prosperity to their marriage.

The broom jumping ceremony may be performed after the wedding vows and before the reception. The couple holds hands and jumps over the broom together, often to the applause and cheers of their guests. This tradition is not only fun and unique, but it also adds a cultural touch to the wedding ceremony. In addition to symbolizing the sweeping away of their old lives, the broom jumping ceremony also represents the couple's willingness to overcome any obstacles that may come their way in their marriage. It is a beautiful tradition, which adds a touch of symbolism and cultural significance to the wedding ceremony.

- *Good fit for: handfasting ceremony, reception*
- *Children or extended family participation: Suitable*
- *Complexity: Easy*

2. Maypole Dancing

Maypole dancing was a common medieval Pagan tradition in Europe, including Slovakia. A tall pole, often adorned with ribbons and flowers, would be erected, and the wedding party and guests would dance around it. This symbolized the renewal of life and the awakening of nature in spring. The maypole itself historically was made from a young tree, stripped of its branches, and decorated with various items such as flowers, ribbons, and sometimes even fruits. The pole was then erected in a central location, often in the village square or a large open field, where everyone could gather around it. The dance itself was a festive and joyous occasion, often accompanied by music and singing. Dancers would form a circle around the pole, each holding a ribbon attached to the top of the pole. As the dance progressed, the dancers would weave in and out, causing the ribbons to intertwine and wrap around the pole. This created a beautiful and colorful pattern on the pole, which was believed to bring good luck and prosperity.

In some regions, the maypole dance was also associated with fertility rites. The pole itself was seen as a phallic symbol, representing the male principle, while the ribbons and flowers symbolized the female principle. The intertwining of the ribbons was seen as a symbolic union of the male and female, which was believed to ensure fertility and abundance for the coming year.

- *Good fit for: engagement party, reception*
- *Children or extended family participation: Suitable*
- *Complexity: Advanced*

3. Jumping over a Fire or Water

Similar to other Pagan traditions, the couple might have been required to jump over a small fire or stream, signifying a purification and a fresh start in their union. This ritual was believed to cleanse the couple of their past mistakes and misfortunes, allowing them to start their new life together with a clean slate. The fire or stream was seen as a barrier between their old life and their new one, and jumping over it symbolized their commitment to leave behind their past and move forward together. In some traditions, the fire was also seen as a symbol of the couple's passion and love for each other. By jumping over it, they were demonstrating their willingness to face any challenges that might come their way, fueled by their love and dedication to each other. The stream, on the other hand, was often seen as a symbol of life and fertility. Jumping over it was believed to bless the couple with a fruitful and prosperous marriage. These rituals were performed in the presence of the community, who would gather to witness and celebrate the couple's union. The couple's successful jump over the fire or stream was often met with cheers and applause, marking the beginning of their new life together.

- *Good fit for: handfasting ceremony, reception, honeymoon*

- *Children or extended family participation: Not Suitable*
- *Complexity: Medium-Advanced*

Slovenia

1. Breaking Bread
In Slovenian Slavic weddings, the couple breaks bread together as a symbol of their unity and shared life journey. The bread may be passed around for the guests to share in the blessing. In Slovenian Slavic weddings, the couple also receives a blessing from their parents and elders. This can be done by the parents placing their hands on the couple's heads and saying a prayer or blessing. The couple then drinks from a shared cup of wine, symbolizing their shared life and commitment to each other.

- *Good fit for: proposal, engagement ceremony, party or dinner, reception, honeymoon*
- *Children or extended family participation: Suitable*
- *Complexity: Easy*

Ukraine

1. Rushnyk Ritual
In Ukraine, a prominent handfasting ritual involves the use of a rushnyk, an embroidered ceremonial cloth. During the

ceremony, the couple stands on the rushnyk, which symbolizes the path they will walk together. It is draped over their shoulders, signifying their unity and the protection it provides. The rushnyk is often decorated with traditional symbols and motifs, each carrying a specific meaning. For instance, the tree of life motif symbolizes fertility and family continuity, while the sun represents health and prosperity.

The couple's hands are also tied together with a rushnyk, symbolizing their commitment and unity. The rushnyk is not only used in weddings, but also in other important life events such as christenings, funerals, and even as a talisman for protection. It is a significant part of Ukrainian culture and tradition, embodying the people's beliefs, hopes, and aspirations.

- *Good fit for: handfasting ceremony*
- *Children or extended family participation: Not Suitable*
- *Complexity: Medium*

2. Korovai Sharing

In Ukrainian Slavic weddings, a korovai (a round, braided bread) is a central element. The korovai is blessed and then shared among the newlyweds and guests, symbolizing the communal support and unity of the couple. The korovai is often elaborately decorated with symbols and motifs having specific meanings. For instance, two birds represent the couple, while other animals symbolize prosperity and fertility. The sun, moon, and stars are also common motifs, symbolizing the divine forces, which guide human life.

The process of making the korovai is a communal activity, often involving the couple's close relatives and friends. It is prepared a few days before the wedding. The process begins with a prayer, asking for blessings and good fortune for the couple. The dough is then kneaded and shaped into a round loaf, which is then decorated with the various symbols.

During the wedding ceremony, the korovai is placed on a rushnyk, a traditional Ukrainian embroidered towel, and is presented to the couple. The couple then breaks the bread, with the person who gets the larger piece considered the head of the family. After the ceremony, the korovai is divided among the guests. This is often done by the godparents or the eldest members of the family, symbolizing the passing on of wisdom and experience. The bread may be served with salt, symbolizing the hardships of life the couple may face together.

- *Good fit for: engagement ceremony, handfasting ceremony, reception*
- *Children or extended family participation: Suitable*
- *Complexity: Easy-Medium*

3. Blessing with Water

As a nod to Ukraine's strong connection with water (rivers, lakes, and the Black Sea), consider having a blessing with water. The couple can dip their hands in a bowl of water or have water sprinkled over them to symbolize purification and a fresh start. This ritual can be performed by the officiant or a close family member. The water can be collected from a significant body of water in Ukraine, such as the Dnieper River or the Black Sea, to add a deeper connection to the country. The person performing the blessing can say something like, "May this water, drawn from the heart of Ukraine, cleanse your past and bless your future. May it remind you of the flow of love and life, always changing, always constant. As these waters nourish the earth, may your love nourish each other." The couple can then dip their hands into the water together, symbolizing their unity and shared commitment to their new life together.

Alternatively, the person performing the blessing can sprinkle the water over the couple, symbolizing a shower of blessings and good wishes. This water blessing can be a beautiful and meaningful addition to a Ukrainian wedding ceremony, connecting the couple to their cultural roots and the natural beauty of their homeland.

- *Good fit for: engagement ceremony, handfasting ceremony, house blessing*
- *Children or extended family participation: Suitable*
- *Complexity: Easy*

These are a few examples of Slavic handfasting rituals from various countries within Eastern Europe. The specific customs and rituals can vary widely, but they all emphasize the couple's commitment, unity, and the importance of community and tradition in celebrating their love.

Recommended Additional Reading:

"Occult Russia: Pagan, Esoteric, and Mystical Traditions" by Christopher McIntosh

"Bulgarian Folk Customs" by Mercia MacDermott

"Native Faith. Polish Neo-Paganism at the Brink of the 21st Century" by Scott Simpson

87

"Native Faith. Polish Neo-Paganism at the Brink of the 21st Century" by Scott Simpson

CHAPTER 5 WICCAN HANDFASTING TRADITIONS

Whimsical Wiccan Wedding

Bathed in the warm glow of a sunlit afternoon, nestled within the heart of California's awe-inspiring redwood forest, Alexa and Morgan, readied themselves to commemorate their profound love and unwavering commitment through the spiritual rite of a Wiccan handfasting ceremony. Their love story had unfolded beneath the tender shelter of these timeless, towering trees. Today, they were poised to honor their deep-seated connection through a sacred union.

Encircled by the comforting presence of cherished friends and family, Alexa and Morgan positioned themselves beneath an exquisitely embellished altar, crafted from an array of local flora, aromatic herbs, and shimmering crystals. The air was perfumed with the calming scents of lavender and sage, setting a serene ambiance as they embarked on their mystical ritual.

Clad in ethereal white gowns, the couple, their heads crowned with garlands of wildflowers, clasped hands and embarked on a sunwise journey around the circle. Sarah, cradling a petite cauldron, wafted the smoky scent of smoldering sage into the air, while Emily brandished a gleaming silver athame, a ceremonial knife. With each measured stride, they wove an unseen circle of potent energy, delineating the hallowed ground where their love would be sanctified.

Turning to face each of the cardinal directions, the couple summoned the elemental forces. Alexa invoked the steadfast spirits of the Earth, while Morgan beckoned the capricious spirits of the Air. United, they called upon the fiery passion of Fire and the soothing calm of Water, inviting these elemental forces to bear witness and bestow their blessings upon their union. In response, the forest whispered its approval through the gentle rustling of leaves and the soft murmur of a nearby brook.

At the center of the circle, Alexa and Morgan stood before their officiant, a wise Wiccan priestess. The priestess held a beautiful cord, braided with colors representing the couple's intentions: love, trust, harmony, and the cycles of nature. With reverence, the priestess wrapped the cord around Alexa and Morgan's joined hands, forming a figure-eight, the symbol of eternity. As she did, she recited a blessing:

"By the power of Earth, I bind you together in love and trust."
"By the power of Air, I bless your communication and harmony."

"By the power of Fire, I ignite your passion and
commitment."
"By the power of Water, I cleanse and renew your spirits."

Gazing deeply into each other's eyes, Alexa and Morgan
poured out their heartfelt vows. Each pledged to be the
other's love and companion and an equal partner
throughout life's unpredictable journey. Emotions ran high,
tears of joy and laughter cascading freely down their cheeks
as they exchanged rings. These weren't ordinary rings, they
were symbols of their love, imbued with the vibrant energy
of the forest where they had spent countless hours together,
and the profound love they held for each other.

Alexa and Morgan's love story began in the heart of the
Amazon rainforest, where they were both working as
environmental scientists. Their shared passion for nature
and conservation brought them together, and they spent
countless hours exploring the forest, conducting research,
and fighting to protect the environment. Their handfasting
ceremony reminded them of the forest where their love had
blossomed. The rings were a symbol of their commitment
not only to each other, but also to the environment. Alexa
and Morgan's vows were promises of love and pledges to
continue their shared mission of environmental
conservation. Their love story serves as a reminder that true
partnership is about more than love; it's about shared values,
mutual respect, and a commitment to making the world a
better place.

The ceremony concluded with a shared feast of locally
sourced wine, followed by dancing beneath the ancient
redwoods. Their friends and family rejoiced, toasting to the

love and happiness of Alexa and Morgan. As the sun set over the redwoods, casting a warm, golden glow on the gathered circle of loved ones, Alexa and Morgan felt the love of the forest, the elements, and each other surround them. Their Wiccan handfasting had united them in a bond transcending time and space, and they knew their love would continue to flourish, like the ancient trees bearing witness to their sacred union.

Wiccan Ceremonies

Wicca is a modern, nature-based Pagan religion, which celebrates the cycles of the earth and the divine in many forms. Emerging in the mid-20th century, Wicca draws inspiration from ancient Pagan practices and folklore, blending these elements with modern spiritual and ceremonial practices. Central to Wiccan belief is the veneration of both the Goddess and the God, often viewed as the Moon Goddess and the Horned God. Wiccans may observe the changing of the seasons through eight major festivals, known collectively as the Wheel of the Year, and many also practice forms of magic, seeing it as a natural extension of the natural world and its energies. Wicca emphasizes personal experience and autonomy in spirituality, encouraging followers to connect with the divine as they understand it. As a highly decentralized religion with many traditions and paths, Wicca allows for a diverse range of practices and beliefs, united by a reverence for nature and a focus on harmony and balance.

Wiccan handfasting ceremonies are highly individualized and can vary significantly from one couple to another. Wicca, as a modern Pagan religion, doesn't have a strict set of standardized rules or tenets for marriage ceremonies. Instead, Wiccan handfasting ceremonies are often tailored to the beliefs and preferences of the couple and the officiant who is conducting the ceremony. Sometimes the handfasting ceremony is used to represent an engagement period for a year and a day, at which time the couple decides if they want to formalize the marriage. This aligns with certain ancient practices.

The attire is often medieval, fairy-themed, witchy, gothic or other Pagan-styled, such as Viking, Celtic or Druid style. Be sure to let guests know the theme on the invitations. The ceremony is normally planned for outdoors to honor nature. As in most modern weddings, the couple often opts to have a wedding cake that the couple cuts together and/or a groom's cake. The cake decorations often reflect the theme of the wedding or the couple's interests.

Wiccan handfastings are typically officiated by Wiccan clergy or individuals who have been trained in Wiccan traditions and are recognized within the Wiccan community, such as Wiccan clergy or individuals who have been trained in Wiccan traditions and are recognized within the Wiccan community. It's essential for the couple to consult with the officiant or clergy member they wish to have conduct the ceremony. They should discuss the specific elements and rituals they want to include, as well as any legal requirements for marriage in their jurisdiction. Additionally, couples should ensure their chosen officiant is recognized and authorized to perform weddings in their area. Also, ask the officiant to what extent the ceremony can be customized.

Here are some common rituals which may be incorporated into Wiccan marriage ceremonies:

1. Invocation of the Elements:
Wiccan ceremonies often begin with the invocation of the four classical elements—Earth, Air, Fire, and Water. This is done to seek blessings and balance from these elemental forces.The invocation of the elements is a way of acknowledging and honoring the fundamental building blocks of the universe. Each element is associated with a particular direction, color, and set of symbolic attributes.

      a. Earth: The element of Earth is associated with the North, the color green, and the qualities of stability, grounding, and physicality. It is often symbolically represented by stones, crystals, or salt.

      b. Air: The element of Air is associated with the East, the color yellow, and the qualities of intellect, communication, and inspiration. It is often symbolically represented by feathers, incense, or bells.

      c. Fire: The element of Fire is associated with the South, the color red, and the qualities of transformation, passion, and will. It is often symbolically represented by candles, wands, or swords.

      d. Water: The element of Water is associated with the West, the color blue, and the qualities of emotion, intuition, and healing. It is often symbolically represented by chalices, bowls of water, or mirrors.

The couple may offer gifts to the elements, such as placing a small bowl of honey or milk for the earth, incense for the air, a candle for the fire, and a bowl of water, as a way to honor the elemental forces.

During the invocation, the Wiccan practitioner often draws a circle to create a sacred space, then call upon each element in turn, inviting it to lend its energy to the ceremony. This is typically done through a combination of spoken words, gestures, and the use of symbolic objects. The invocation of the elements is a way of connecting with the natural world, aligning oneself with the cycles of nature, and drawing upon the power of the elements to manifest one's intentions. It is a fundamental part of Wiccan ritual and a powerful tool for spiritual growth and transformation.

- *Good fit for: engagement ceremony or party, bridal shower, handfasting ceremony*
- *Children or extended family participation: Suitable*
- *Complexity: Easy-Medium*

2. Casting of the Circle:

Wiccan ceremonies often involve the casting of a sacred circle to create a consecrated and protected space for the ceremony to take place. The circle may be cast with a ritual knife, called an athame, or a wand. The four cardinal directions (as described above) are often invoked in this process. The circle is seen as a boundary between the physical world and the spiritual realm and serves to keep out negative energies or entities. The circle symbolizes the continuous cycle of birth, death, and rebirth, as well as the interconnectedness of all things. The circle also helps to contain and focus the energy raised during the ceremony.

Once the circle is cast, the ceremony can begin. This may involve various rituals, such as the invocation of deities, spell casting, divination, or the celebration of a sabbat (Wiccan holiday). The specific activities depend on the purpose of the ceremony. After the ceremony is complete, the circle is closed in a respectful manner, thanking the elements and any deities that were invoked. This is often done by reversing the process used to cast the circle. Practices can vary widely among Wiccans, and not all use a circle or follow these exact steps. Some may prefer to use a different method for creating sacred space or may not feel the need to use one at all.

The ceremony concludes with the closing of the sacred circle, releasing the energies raised and ending the ritual. The circular shape of the casting and closing of the circle reflects the cyclical and seasonal nature of many Pagan and Wiccan belief systems. Closing the circle is a way to show respect to the divine forces, the spirits of the land, and any deities or energies invoked during the ritual. Closing the circle acknowledges that the sacred space is no longer needed and allows for the respectful release of any energies that were raised. The specific method of closing the circle can vary among Wiccan traditions and individual practitioners. Some may use a simple gesture or visualization, while others may recite specific words or perform specific actions to close the circle.

- *Good fit for: anytime a circle was previously opened*
- *Children or extended family participation: Not Suitable*
- *Complexity: Easy – Medium*

3. Calling on Deities:

Many Wiccans choose to call upon specific deities or invoke the God and Goddess as witnesses and blessings upon the union. The deities chosen can vary based on the couple's tradition or personal beliefs. For example, some Wiccans may choose to call upon the Horned God and/or the Triple Goddess, who are often seen as the primary deities in Wicca. The Horned God represents the masculine aspect of divinity and is associated with nature, wilderness, sexuality, hunting, and the life cycle. The Triple Goddess represents the feminine aspect of divinity and is associated with the moon, magic, witchcraft, the mystery of death and rebirth, and fertility. Other Wiccans may choose to call upon specific deities from various pantheons. For example, a couple might choose to invoke Aphrodite and Eros for their association with love and passion, or Freya and Freyr for their association with fertility and prosperity.

- *Good fit for: proposal, engagement ceremony or party, bridal shower, handfasting ceremony*
- *Children or extended family participation: Suitable*
- *Complexity: Easy – Medium*

Additional Wiccan Rituals

Wiccan handfasting ceremonies can be highly personalized, and couples often incorporate unique rituals or elements holding special meaning to them. Here are some additional unique Wiccan rituals and elements, which couples may choose to include in their handfasting ceremony. Note many of these originate with rituals covered in Part 1 from various cultures.

1. Jumping the Broom and /or Fire:
The couple jumps over a broom together as a symbol of sweeping away the old and stepping into a new life together. It's a way of marking the threshold of their new life together. A contemporary tradition involves leaping over a fire, followed immediately by a jump over a broom. This ritual is believed to symbolize the burning away of past negative influences through the purifying power of fire. Frequently, the Handfasting cord, a significant symbol of unity in marriage, is attached to the broom. This broom, adorned with the cord, is then prominently displayed in the couple's home as a constant reminder of their commitment and shared journey.

- *Good fit for: handfasting ceremony, reception*
- *Children or extended family participation: Suitable*
- *Complexity: Easy*

2. Ancestral Honoring:
Couples may choose to honor their ancestors by lighting candles, making offerings on an ancestral altar, or reciting prayers to invite the blessings and guidance of their forebears. Before the ceremony, the couple should research their family histories to identify specific ancestors they wish to honor. This can include grandparents, parents, or other significant family members who have passed away.
  Honoring items or symbols represent the ancestors you wish to honor. These could be photographs, heirlooms, candles, incense, or other meaningful objects associated with your family heritage.

Many Wiccans believe in the importance of connecting with their ancestral heritage as a way to understand their roots and cultural background. The joining of two families is of great significance in altering the future state of each family's heritage. Honoring ancestors during a handfasting ceremony is a way to acknowledge the lineage and traditions, which have shaped the couple's identity and spirituality. Recognizing and honoring ancestors reinforces the idea of continuity and the cycle of life. It acknowledges that the love and commitment of the couple are part of a larger tapestry of family and heritage, and it symbolizes the passing of traditions, values, and blessings from one generation to the next.

Wiccans often view their ancestors as spiritual guides and guardians. By honoring them, the couple seeks their wisdom, blessings, and protection as they embark on a new phase of life together. Ancestors are seen as a source of ancestral knowledge and collective wisdom, which can be called upon for guidance.

- *Good fit for: family engagement dinner, bridal shower, rehearsal dinner, handfasting ceremony, reception*
- *Children or extended family participation: Suitable*
- *Complexity: Easy*

3. Blessing Stones:
Guests can be given stones to hold and imbue with their well-wishes and blessings for the couple. These stones can later be placed on an altar or in a special container as a reminder of the love and support of friends and family. This is a beautiful and symbolic way to involve guests in the wedding ceremony. The stones can be of any type, but it's

often nice to choose ones holding special meaning or significance to the couple. For example, they could be stones from a place that's important to them, or stones associated with certain qualities or virtues, like love, strength, or resilience.

Before the ceremony, the stones can be placed in a basket or other container and handed out to guests as they arrive. The officiant can explain the purpose of the stones and invite guests to hold them in their hands during the ceremony, imbuing them with their well-wishes and blessings for the couple. After the ceremony, the stones can be collected and placed on an altar or in a special container. This can be done by the couple themselves, or by a designated person. The stones serve as a tangible reminder of the love and support of their friends and family and can be kept in a special place in their home. This ritual can be adapted in many ways to suit the couple's preferences and beliefs. For example, they could choose to use crystals instead of stones, or they could invite guests to write their wishes on the stones with a special marker. The important thing is that the ritual reflects the couple's unique love story and the community of support around them.

- *Good fit for: engagement party, handfasting ceremony, reception*
- *Children or extended family participation: Suitable*
- *Complexity: Easy*

4. Exchange of Ancestral Gifts:
The couple may exchange symbolic gifts representing their family heritage or personal histories, reflecting their commitment to honoring each other's roots. These gifts can

range from traditional items like jewelry or clothing to more unique items like a family heirloom or a piece of art. For example, a bride with Irish heritage might give her groom a Claddagh ring, symbolizing love, loyalty, and friendship. A groom with Japanese ancestry might present his bride with a traditional Japanese kimono, representing beauty and grace. These gifts not only honor the couple's individual backgrounds but also symbolize the blending of their two families. They serve as a tangible reminder of the couple's commitment to respect and cherish each other's heritage as they build a new life together.

In addition to traditional gifts, some couples choose to exchange items reflecting their personal histories. For example, a couple who met while hiking might exchange compasses, symbolizing their shared love of adventure and their commitment to navigating life's challenges together. A couple who bonded over their love of music might exchange mixtapes of songs having special meaning to them. Regardless of the specific items exchanged, the act of giving and receiving symbolic gifts is a powerful way for couples to express their love and commitment to each other. This tradition adds depth and meaning to the wedding ceremony, making it a truly personal and memorable event.

- *Good fit for: family engagement dinner, rehearsal dinner, handfasting ceremony, reception*
- *Children or extended family participation: Suitable*
- *Complexity: Easy – Medium*

5. Herb Blessing:
Herbs and flowers with symbolic or magical properties may be used in the ceremony, either as decorations, as part of the

handfasting cord, or in a blessing ritual. For example, rosemary can represent love and remembrance. See chapter 9 on symbolism.

- *Good fit for: proposal, engagement ceremony or party, bridal shower, bachelorette party, bachelor party, handfasting ceremony, reception*
- *Children or extended family participation: Suitable*
- *Complexity: Easy*

6. Divination:

Couples may opt to integrate mystical elements such as tarot cards, runes, or a crystal ball into their wedding ceremony. They do this not only to add a unique touch to their special day, but also to glean potential insights into their shared future or to seek spiritual guidance for their journey together. These mystical elements can be incorporated in various ways. For instance, a tarot reader can be invited to perform a reading for the couple, providing them with insights about their future together. The tarot cards can also be used as a form of entertainment for the guests during the reception.

Runes, on the other hand, can be used in the handfasting ceremony itself. The couple can choose specific runes symbolizing their hopes and dreams for their marriage, and these can be incorporated into their vows or used as part of the wedding decor. A crystal ball can be used in a similar way. The couple can have a psychic or medium perform a crystal ball reading during the ceremony, providing them with guidance and insights about their future. Alternatively, the crystal ball can be used as a centerpiece at the reception, adding a mystical touch to the decor. Moreover, they can provide the couple with valuable insights and guidance for their journey together, making their wedding day even more special and meaningful.

- *Good fit for: proposal, engagement ceremony or party, bridal shower, bachelorette party, bachelor party, handfasting ceremony, reception*
- *Children or extended family participation: Suitable*
- *Complexity: Medium- Advanced*

7. Libation Ceremony:
The couple can pour libations of wine or another beverage into a shared chalice as a symbol of their union and their willingness to share all aspects of their lives. This ritual can be performed during the wedding ceremony, often after the exchange of vows and rings. The couple each takes a turn pouring their chosen beverage into the chalice, symbolizing the blending of their individual lives into one shared journey.

The libation ceremony can be customized to fit the couple's personal beliefs and traditions. For example, they may choose to pour red and white wine to symbolize the blending of their individual personalities, or they may choose a beverage holding personal significance to them. The couple then drinks from the shared chalice, further symbolizing their unity and shared commitment. This act can be accompanied by a blessing or a toast, often delivered by the officiant or a loved one. The libation ceremony is a beautiful and symbolic way to celebrate the union of two individuals, and it can add a unique and personal touch to any wedding ceremony.

- *Good fit for: proposal, engagement ceremony or party, bridal shower, bachelorette party, bachelor party, handfasting ceremony, reception*
- *Children or extended family participation: Not Suitable*
- *Complexity: Easy*

Remember, the most meaningful elements to include in a handfasting ceremony are those that resonate with the couple's beliefs, values, and personal connection. These unique rituals can add depth and personal significance to the ceremony, making it a truly special and memorable experience for the couple and their guests.

Wicca is a highly flexible and individualized religion, and each Wiccan or Wiccan couple may have their own unique beliefs and practices. The key tenets of a Wiccan marriage ceremony often revolve around love, commitment, balance, and the celebration of nature and the divine in all things. Couples may choose to incorporate or omit various elements based on their personal beliefs and preferences.

Recommended Additional Reading:
"Seasons of Wicca: The Essential Guide to Rituals and Rites to Enhance Your Spiritual Journey" by <u>Ambrosia Hawthorn</u>

PART 2
DISCOVERING CUSTOMIZATION
FOR THE PAGAN IN YOU

CHAPTER 6 NON-TRADITIONAL RITUALS FOR INDIVIDUALS

Have you ever wondered how to make your handfasting ceremony unique and personal? The answer lies in customized rituals. In Part 1 of the book, we explored many long-lived rituals, which can easily be incorporated into your handfasting events. Most of these are deployed at the handfasting ceremony itself or the reception. With a few customizations you can transform those activities into rituals for other events leading up to the handfasting. Part 2 we delve into non-traditional rituals I designed for use by individuals, couples and groups to customize your experience throughout the series of handfasting events. See more about customizing rituals yourself in Chapter 9.

Finally, refer to Chapter 11 Mastering the Art of Sacred Union for weaving all the pieces together. Select rituals that reflect your personal beliefs and values to create a memorable experience.

Rituals for Individuals

The couple is often enveloped in a myriad of rituals and ceremonies tailored specifically for them as a unit. But what about the individual partners? Rituals centered around the individual can serve as a powerful recognition of their distinct identities and roles. They can bring healing to the individual so they enter the marriage with a healed spirit. They also provide a meaningful way to commemorate the conclusion of their single life chapter, marking the transition with respect and honor. Here are some examples of rituals for individuals, which you may include as part of a larger event or ceremony or on its own.

The List:

1. Love Draw
2. Purification Ritual Bath
3. Release
4. Divination Ritual for Insight
5. Ancestral Healing
6. Akashic Healing
7. Womb Blessing or Womb Steaming
8. Henna Sigils
9. Mourn
10. Thrive

1. Love Draw Ritual

Purpose: To deepen the bond and attraction between partners before their handfasting ceremony.

Materials:
- Pink Candle (for love and affection)- Red Candle (for passion and strength of love)
- White Candle (for purity of intention and new beginnings)
- Rose Quartz (for unconditional love)
- Piece of Paper and Pen- Rose Petals (for romance and love)
- Lavender (for peace and harmony)- A small bowl of water (representing emotional connection)
- Incense (choose a scent associated with love, like jasmine or ylang-ylang which are strongly scented flowers)

Preparation:
- Choose a quiet and comfortable space where you won't be disturbed.
- Cleanse the area and yourself to remove any negative energy. This can be done with smudging sage or simply visualizing a bright light purifying the space and yourself.
- Arrange the candles in a triangle on your altar or sacred space. Place the rose quartz at the center.

Ritual Steps:

1. Set Your Intention: Sit quietly and focus on your intention to deepen the love and connection with your partner. Visualize your upcoming handfasting, filled with love, understanding, and harmony.
2. Candle Lighting: Light the pink candle and say, "With this light, I draw love and affection." Light the red candle and say, "With this light, I ignite passion

and a strong bond." Light the white candle and say, "With this light, I affirm pure intentions and new beginnings."

3. Love Affirmation: Write a love affirmation or poem for your partner on the piece of paper. It should express your deepest feelings and commitment. Fold the paper and place it under the rose quartz.

4. Rose Petals and Lavender Offering: Sprinkle rose petals and lavender around the candles and rose quartz, affirming your wish for a romantic and harmonious union.

5. Water Blessing: Dip your fingers in the bowl of water and sprinkle a few drops around the candles, saying, "With this water, I nurture and deepen our emotional bond."

6. Incense Burning: Light the incense, allowing the fragrance to fill the space, symbolizing the spreading of your love and intentions.

7. Meditation and Visualization: Meditate for a few minutes, visualizing a strong, loving, and harmonious relationship with your partner. Feel the energy from the candles and rose quartz enveloping you with warmth and love.

8. Closing the Ritual: Once your meditation is complete, express gratitude to the divine, the elements, and the universe for supporting your love. Extinguish the candles safely.

9. Post-Ritual: Keep the rose quartz with you or in a special place until the day of your handfasting. Carry the affirmation or poem with you during the ceremony or read it to your partner as part of your vows.

This Love Draw Ritual is a meaningful way to spiritually connect with your partner before the handfasting, reinforcing the intentions and love you share.

- *Good fit for: individual private moment, bridal shower, bachelorette party or bachelor party*
- *Children or extended family participation: Not Suitable*
- *Complexity: Easy*

2. Purification Ritual Bath

Purpose: To cleanse and purify the spirit, and to promote relaxation and clarity before the handfasting ceremony.

Materials:
- Bathtub filled with warm water
- Sea Salt or Epsom Salt (for purification and grounding)
- Essential Oils (lavender for relaxation, rose for love, or frankincense for spiritual connection)
- Herbs or Flowers (like rose petals, lavender, or chamomile for calming and loving energy)
- White Candle (symbolizing purity and new beginnings)- Incense or Smudging Stick (like sage or palo santo for cleansing)
- Crystals (optional - such as clear quartz for clarity, amethyst for peace, or rose quartz for love)
- Soft, meditative music or nature sounds (optional)

Preparation:
- Cleanse the bathroom space beforehand, either physically by tidying and cleaning, or spiritually through smudging.

- Draw a bath with warm water, adding sea salt or Epsom salt, a few drops of your chosen essential oils, and herbs or flower petals.
- Place the white candle and crystals (if using) around the bathtub.
- Light the candle and incense or smudging stick.

Ritual Steps:

1. Set Your Intention: Before entering the bath, take a moment to set your intention for purification and peace. Focus on releasing any stress, negativity, or worries.
2. Cleansing Smudge: If using incense or a smudging stick, wave the smoke around your body, starting from the head and moving downwards, envisioning any negative energy being cleansed away. You can also diffuse essential oils or mix them with water in a spray bottle for the same purpose.
3. Meditation and Visualization: Slowly step into the bath, allowing yourself to become enveloped by the warm, fragrant water. Close your eyes and take deep, soothing breaths. While in the bath, meditate on the water cleansing not just your body but your spirit. Visualize any negativity, stress, or tension washing away. Imagine a pure, radiant light enveloping you, filling you with peace, love, and joy.
4. Affirmations: You may choose to recite affirmations or simple mantras such as, "I am cleansed, I am pure, I am calm," or, "I welcome love, joy, and new beginnings."
5. Closing the Ritual: When you feel ready, slowly rise from the bath, envisioning yourself emerging renewed and purified, ready for your handfasting

ceremony. Extinguish the candle and incense safely. Thank any deities, spirits, or elements you feel connected with for their guidance and cleansing.

6. Post-Bath: After drying off, take time to relax, perhaps by dressing in clean, comfortable clothes, meditating, or simply resting in a peaceful space. Reflect on the ritual and your feelings. Carry the sense of peace and purity with you as you approach your handfasting ceremony.

This purification ritual bath is designed to be a calming and cleansing experience, providing a sacred moment of solitude and reflection before one of life's significant milestones.

- *Good fit for: individual private moment pre-handfasting*
- *Children or extended family participation: Not Suitable*
- *Complexity: Easy*

3. Release Ritual

Purpose: To release negative energies, emotions, past hurts, or any blocks to a successful and harmonious marriage.

Materials:
- A quiet, comfortable, and private space
- A small fire-safe bowl or cauldron- Strips of paper and a pen
- A lighter or matches
- Smudging herbs (like sage, lavender, or palo santo) or incense
- A small piece of rose quartz or amethyst (for love and healing)

- A small bowl of water (for emotional healing and purification)
- A white or black candle (white for new beginnings, black for absorbing negativity)

Preparation: Cleanse your space physically and spiritually. This could involve tidying the area, then smudging with your chosen herb or incense to clear the space of negative energy.

Ritual Steps:
1. Set Your Intention: Sit quietly in your space, holding the intention in your heart to release anything that no longer serves you or could hinder your marriage.
2. Light the Candle: Light the white or black candle, focusing on its flame as a symbol of transformation and renewal.
3. Writing Release Statements: On the strips of paper, write down any negative energies, emotions or potential blocks to the success of your marriage that you wish to release. Be as specific as you can, acknowledging each item without judgment.
4. Smudging: Use the smudging herbs or incense to purify yourself and the space around you. Wave the smoke over your body and around the written strips, envisioning the removal of negative energy.
5. Burning Ceremony: One by one, take each strip of paper, read it aloud or silently, acknowledging its release, and then burn it in the fire-safe bowl or cauldron. As the paper burns, imagine the negative energy being transformed into light and positivity. After each strip is burned, say, "I release what no

longer serves me" or a similar phrase that resonates with you.

6. Crystal and Water for Healing: Hold the rose quartz or amethyst and allow yourself to feel the healing energy. You may wish to place it over your heart. Dip your fingers in the bowl of water and lightly sprinkle some on yourself, signifying emotional healing and purification.

7. Meditation and Visualization: Spend a few minutes in meditation, visualizing yourself filled with light and surrounded by peace. Imagine a bright future in your marriage, free from the burdens you've released.

8. Closing the Ritual: Extinguish the candle safely. Express gratitude to the universe, deities, spirits, or elements that you feel connected with for their support in this process.

9. Grounding: To conclude, do a simple grounding exercise, such as eating something light, walking barefoot on the earth, or visualizing roots growing from your feet into the ground.

10. Post-Ritual: Keep the crystal with you as a reminder of your commitment to release and heal. Discard the ashes in a way that feels meaningful and respectful, such as burying them or letting them be carried away by a stream of water.

This release ritual is a powerful way to consciously let go of any negative influences or past issues, paving the way for a positive and fulfilling marriage.

- *Good fit for: individual private moment*
- *Children or extended family participation: Not Suitable*
- *Complexity: Easy*

4. Divination Ritual for Insight

Purpose: To seek guidance and insights from the universe or the divine about three things needed for a successful first year of marriage.

Materials:
- A deck of oracle cards
- A white candle (for clarity and purity)
- A journal and a pen (for recording insights)
- An optional small crystal for intuition (like amethyst or moonstone)

Preparation: Find a quiet space where you won't be disturbed. Cleanse the area if you wish, using smudging herbs or by visualizing a bright light purifying the space. Sit comfortably and place the deck of oracle cards, the white candle, and the crystal (if using) in front of you.

Ritual Steps:
1. Set Your Intention: Light the white candle and take a few deep breaths to center yourself. Focus on your intention to receive clear and helpful insights for your first year of marriage.
2. Connect with the Deck: Hold the oracle cards in your hands. If you have a specific deity, ancestor, or spirit guide you work with, you may call upon them for guidance. If not, simply ask the universe for clear and loving guidance.
3. Shuffle the Cards: While focusing on your intention, shuffle the oracle cards. Trust your intuition to tell you when to stop.

4. Draw Three Cards: Draw three cards from the deck. Lay them out in front of you in the order they were drawn. These represent three key insights for your first year of marriage.

5. Interpret the Cards: Look at each card and note your first impressions and feelings. Pay attention to the imagery, symbols, and the message of the card. Reflect on how each card's message applies to your upcoming marriage. The first card may represent an essential quality or strength to cultivate. The second card could symbolize a challenge to be aware of or overcome. The third card might suggest an action to take or an area to focus on. Refer to the booklet that comes with the Oracle card deck for further guidance on interpreting the cards.

6. Journal Your Insights: Write down the cards you drew and your interpretations in your journal. Reflect on how these insights can be integrated into your marriage journey.

7. Closing the Ritual: Thank your deity, spirit guides, or the universe for their guidance. Extinguish the candle safely. Spend a few moments in quiet contemplation, absorbing the insights and the peace of the ritual.

8. Post-Ritual Reflection: In the days following the ritual, keep your journal handy. Reflect on the insights you received and how you can apply them to your marriage. Keep the insights you gained in mind as you enter your marriage. Consider revisiting your journal throughout your first year of marriage to remind yourself of the guidance you received.

This divination ritual is a thoughtful way to seek spiritual guidance and prepare yourself internally for the journey of marriage. Remember, the insights from oracle cards are interpretative and should be used as guidance rather than absolute truths.

- *Good fit for: individual private moment, bridal shower, bachelorette party or bachelor party*
- *Children or extended family participation: while intended for the individual, you could involve your child/ children and have them draw their own card*
- *Complexity: Medium*

5. Ancestral Healing

Purpose: To connect with the wind spirits and ancestors for healing and clearing of ancestral energies that could affect the marriage.

Materials:
- A quiet outdoor space where the wind can be felt
- A feather (symbolizing air and connection to the wind spirits)
- Small biodegradable offerings (such as flowers, herbs, or seeds)
- A white or blue candle (representing air and spiritual clarity)
- A bell or chime or a wind whistle
- A photograph, memento or symbol representing your ancestors
- A bowl of water (symbolizing emotional healing and cleansing)

Preparation: Choose a time where the wind is present, preferably in a natural and quiet outdoor setting. Set up a small altar facing the direction of the wind with the candle, feather, offerings, bell or chime, photograph or memento, and bowl of water.

Ritual Steps:
1. Setting the Space: Begin by lighting the candle to symbolize the start of the ritual. Hold the feather in your hand, feeling its connection to the wind and air.
2. Invoking the Wind Spirits: Call upon the spirits of the wind to aid in your ancestral healing. You might say, "Spirits of the wind, keepers of wisdom and carriers of the ancestors' voices, I call upon you."
3. Ancestral Acknowledgment: Hold the photograph, memento or symbol, acknowledging your ancestors. Speak of your intention to heal any negative energies or burdens (karmic debt, soul level contracts, spiritual attachments, or other negative energies) passed down through your lineage.
4. Offering and Bell Ringing: Place your offerings on the altar as a gesture of goodwill to the spirits and ancestors. Ring the bell or chime to signal your respect and readiness to receive their guidance and healing.
5. Connecting with the Wind: Stand with your arms open, facing the wind. Blow into your wind whistle or through your hands. Allow the wind to pass over you, envisioning it carrying away ancestral burdens, karmic debts, and negative attachments.
6. Water Cleansing: Dip your fingers in the bowl of water and sprinkle it over the altar and yourself, symbolizing emotional cleansing and purity.
7. Healing Affirmation: Recite an affirmation or prayer for healing, such as, "I release the ancestral burdens

and energies that do not serve the highest good for myself and my future family. May our lineage be healed and purified."

8. Closing the Ritual: Thank the wind spirits and your ancestors for their presence and healing. Extinguish the candle to symbolize the completion of the ritual. Leave the offerings at the site or in nature as a gift to the earth and the spirits.

9. Post-Ritual Reflection: Spend some time in meditation or quiet reflection, absorbing the energy of the ritual and the healing that has begun. In the days following the ritual, be mindful of any changes in your emotions or insights which may arise as a result of this ancestral healing. Consider keeping a journal to document any thoughts, dreams, or shifts in your well-being.

This ritual is a powerful way to connect with the elemental power of the wind for ancestral healing, creating a clear and positive foundation for your upcoming handfasting and marriage.

- *Good fit for: individual private moment*
- *Children or extended family participation: You could get do this with other family members*
- *Complexity: Advanced*

6. Akashic Healing

Purpose: To access the Akashic Records for deep soul-level healing, ensuring they enter the marriage as a spiritually whole and healed partner.

Materials: A quiet, comfortable space for meditation- A journal and pen for recording insights and reflections- Crystals associated with spiritual insight, such as amethyst, clear quartz, or lapis lazuli- Relaxing, meditative music (optional)- A white or purple candle (symbolizing spiritual connection and transformation)- A small bowl of water (for purification)

Preparation: Create a sacred space in a quiet area where you will not be disturbed. This could be an altar or a simple, clean space in your home. Arrange your crystals, candle, and water around you. Light the candle to signify the beginning of the ritual. Turn on the meditative music if you choose to use it.

Ritual Steps:
1. Setting Your Intention: Sit comfortably and take a few deep breaths to center yourself. Set the intention to access your Akashic Records for soul-level healing and clarity.
2. Activation and Invocation for Accessing the Akashic Records:

   Accessing one's Akashic Records may involve a process of energetic and spiritual activation, where the individual attunes themselves to the vibrational frequency of the Akashic realm. This is often achieved through meditation, intention setting, and sometimes the use of specific prayers or invocations. The key is to approach the Akashic Records with a clear intention, respect, and an open heart. Here's your activation process to access the Akashic Records:

"Within the sacred space of my heart and mind, I now set the intention to access my Akashic Records for wisdom, guidance, and healing. I call upon the guardians and keepers of the Akashic Records to assist me in this journey.

Visualize a gentle, radiant light surrounding you, symbolizing the protective and pure energy of the Akashic realm.
In the realm of infinite knowledge and divine memory, I seek access to my soul's records. With respect and clarity of purpose, I ask to be aligned with the highest vibrational frequency of truth and understanding.

Pause and take a deep breath, envisioning yourself becoming attuned to a higher vibrational frequency.

As I enter my Akashic Records, I am open to receiving the wisdom and lessons needed at this time in my life. I trust in the guidance provided and vow to use this knowledge for my highest good and the highest good of all involved.

With gratitude and a heart open to divine insight, I cross the threshold into the realm of the Akashic Records."

Pause for a moment to feel the shift in energy as you connect with your Akashic Records. You may visualize a door opening, a library, a book unfolding, or simply sense a change in your intuitive perception.

"I am now within my Akashic Records. I am ready to receive the wisdom and healing held within. I seek guidance and insight for my highest good and for the highest good of all involved."

3. Receiving Insights and Healing: Ask to be shown any past experiences, traumas, patterns, or karmic debts that need healing before entering your marriage. Pay attention to any images, feelings, or messages that come to you. These may provide insights into what needs to be healed or released. If challenging memories or emotions arise, acknowledge them without judgment and ask for healing and resolution.

4. Affirmation of Release and Healing: - Speak an affirmation of release and healing, such as, "I release any patterns or traumas that no longer serve me. I embrace healing and wholeness in preparation for my handfasting and marriage."

5. Closing the Akashic Records: Offer gratitude for the guidance and healing received. Then, visualize closing the book or door to your Akashic Records, signifying the end of the session. Extinguish the candle to symbolize the closing of your ritual.

6. Journaling Insights: After your meditation, write down any insights, messages, or understandings you received in your journal. Reflect on how these can inform your healing process.

7. Water Purification: Dip your fingers in the bowl of water and sprinkle some on yourself, symbolizing purification and emotional cleansing.

8. Post-Ritual: Take some time to ground yourself. This might involve eating something, spending time in nature, or engaging in a grounding meditation. Reflect on the experience and how you can integrate

the healing into your daily life. Be open to any further insights or shifts that may occur in the days following the ritual.

This ritual is an advanced, powerful tool for accessing the Akashic Records for personal healing, ensuring you are spiritually prepared for your handfasting and the journey of marriage ahead.

- *Good fit for: individual private moment*
- *Children or extended family participation: Not Suitable*
- *Complexity: Advanced*

7. Womb Blessing

A ritual blessing for womb healing is suitable for either the bride or groom, as both can engage in the spiritual healing of their womb space.

Purpose: To cleanse, heal, and honor the spiritual womb, fostering a sense of renewal and preparation for the handfasting.

Materials:
- Healing herbs and beautiful flowers, such as lavender, rose petals, chamomile, yarrow or flowers from your yard
- A white or red candle (white for purity and healing, red for the womb's power and creativity)
- Crystals associated with healing and feminine energy, such as moonstone or rose quartz
- A comfortable place to sit or a meditation cushion
- Soft, soothing music (optional)

Preparation: Create sacred space by lighting the candle and set up your crystals and herbs around your sitting area. Play soothing music if desired.

Ritual Steps:
1. Setting Intentions: Sit comfortably, taking deep breaths. Focus on your intention to heal and honor your womb space. Light the candle, acknowledging the start of a sacred practice.
2. Meditation and Visualization: Close your eyes and place your hands over your womb area (lower abdomen). Visualize a warm, healing light emanating from your hands, filling your womb with energy, cleansing, and healing. Imagine any past traumas, fears, or negative energies dissolving and being replaced by love, strength, and creativity.
3. Place flowers and herbs over your womb space (or on your lower abdomen if you do not have a physical womb) and hold there with your hands.
4. Affirmations: Speak affirmations that resonate with healing and empowerment. For example, "I honor and heal my womb. I release what no longer serves me and welcome new beginnings and joy."
5. Crystal Healing: Hold the crystals, imbuing them with your intentions. Place them on your womb area, feeling their energy aiding in healing and balance.
6. Closing the Ritual: Offer gratitude to the Earth, universe, the divine, or any deities/spirits you work with for their guidance and healing. Extinguish the candle, symbolizing the completion of the ritual. Journal any feelings or insights which arose during the ritual.

7. Post-Ritual: Spend some time in relaxation, allowing the healing process to integrate. You might want to engage in gentle activities like walking in nature or practicing yoga.

Remember, the focus of this ritual is on spiritual and emotional healing. Additional resources: the 13th Rite of the Munay Ki is a powerful womb blessing that you may want to investigate.

- *Good fit for: individual private moment, bridal shower, bachelorette party or bachelor party*
- *Children or extended family participation: could do with other wedding party participants, such as bridesmaids*
- *Complexity: Easy*

8. Henna Sigils

Henna powder can be used to draw powerful spiritual marks, sigils, or symbols on the body, serving as a form of spiritual adornment and protection for the handfasting ceremony. Henna tattoos are non-invasive, last about a week and wear off naturally. Before doing this, ensure you are not allergic to henna. Perform this ritual a day or two prior to the handfasting ceremony.

Purpose: To adorn the body with henna as a sacred act, drawing symbols, sigils, and marks which hold spiritual significance and power, in preparation for the handfasting ceremony.

Materials:
- Natural henna prepared paste (ensure it's from a reliable source and skin-safe)
- Stencils or designs for spiritual symbols, sigils, or meaningful patterns
- A white candle (for purity and spiritual connection)
- Incense or essential oils (for creating a sacred atmosphere)
- Soft, meditative music (optional)
- A mirror (for self-application or to view the designs)
- Lemon juice and sugar mix (to seal the henna)

Preparation: Set up your space in a quiet area where you won't be disturbed. Light the candle and incense, and play meditative music if desired. Lay out your henna, designs/stencils, mirror, and lemon juice/sugar mix. Cleanse the areas of your body where you will apply the henna.

Ritual Steps:
1. Setting Intentions: Sit comfortably, taking deep breaths to center yourself. Focus on your intention for the henna application – protection, love, spiritual connection, etc. Light the candle to symbolize the start of a sacred act.
2. Design Selection: Choose the designs or symbols resonating with your spiritual intentions. These could be traditional wedding symbols, sigils for protection and love, or patterns holding personal meaning.
3. Application of Henna: Begin applying the henna to your skin, either freehand or using stencils. As you draw each symbol, focus on its meaning and your intentions. If you are not comfortable applying henna yourself, you can have a friend or a

professional apply it while maintaining a meditative and respectful atmosphere.

4. Meditation and Visualization: As the henna dries, meditate on the symbols' significance. Visualize them empowering and protecting you during your handfasting ceremony. Consider each mark as a blessing and affirmation of your intentions for the marriage.

5. Sealing the Henna: Once the henna has partially dried, dab the lemon juice and sugar mix over it. This helps to seal the design and darken the stain.

6. Closing the Ritual: Once you have finished applying and sealing the henna, sit quietly for a few moments, absorbing the energy of the ritual. - Extinguish the candle, symbolizing the end of the ritual.

7. Post-Application Care: Allow the henna to remain on your skin for several hours or overnight for the best results. Avoid water in the area to ensure a long-lasting stain. In the following days, as you wear the henna, let it remind you of your intentions and the spiritual protection it offers. Carry these blessings with you into your handfasting ceremony.

The henna designs serve as a beautiful and powerful spiritual adornment during your handfasting, embodying the intentions and energies you've infused into them.

- *Good fit for: individual private moment 1-2 days prior to wedding*
- *Children or extended family participation: You could get some help from a family member or wedding party*
- *Complexity: Medium – Advanced*

9. Mourning Ritual

Purpose: To acknowledge and honor the end of single life and childhood, allowing for a moment of mourning and reflection before stepping into the new chapter of married life.

Materials:
- A small candle (to symbolize the light of the past and the transition to the future)
- Photographs or mementos representing different stages of life (childhood, adolescence, young adulthood)
- A journal and pen (for reflection and recording thoughts)
- A bowl of water (representing emotional cleansing and purification)
- A piece of cloth or ribbon (symbolizing the life being left behind)

Preparation: Set up a small space where you can sit comfortably and won't be disturbed. Arrange the photographs or mementos, the candle, the bowl of water, and the cloth or ribbon before you.

Ritual Steps:
1. Creating Sacred Space: Begin by lighting the candle, acknowledging the sacredness of this moment and the transformation it represents.
2. Reflection: Spend a few moments looking at the photographs or mementos. Allow yourself to reminisce about the memories, experiences, and lessons each represents.

3. Writing Exercise: In your journal, write down what you are mourning – the end of your single life, the aspects of your childhood or past you are leaving behind. Acknowledge the growth, the joys, and even the sorrows.

4. Ritual Mourning: Hold the piece of cloth or ribbon in your hands. As you think about your transition, tie knots in the cloth or ribbon, each representing a significant part of your life which you are now ready to leave behind.

5. Water Cleansing: Dip your fingers in the bowl of water and sprinkle some onto the cloth or ribbon and over yourself, symbolizing emotional cleansing and purification from your past.

6. Farewell and Release: Speak aloud or silently a goodbye to each stage of life you are leaving. It might be something like, "I honor and say goodbye to my childhood, my adolescence, and my years as a single adult. I cherish these memories and lessons as I step forward, transforming into a new beginning."

7. Closing the Ritual: Extinguish the candle, symbolizing the completion of this chapter of life. Take a deep breath, feeling the weight of the past lifting and the readiness for the new journey of marriage.

8. Post-Ritual Reflection: Spend some time in quiet reflection or meditation, contemplating the new path ahead. Keep the cloth or ribbon as a keepsake or respectfully dispose of it, symbolizing the release of your past. Use your journal entries as a reminder of your journey and the growth that has led you to this point.

Mourning rituals provide a structured way to process complex emotions associated with major life changes. This can include sadness, fear, or a sense of loss for the independence or lifestyle that is changing. By addressing these emotions, individuals can enter into marriage with a clearer, more focused mind. This ritual provides a meaningful way to honor and mourn the life stages which have passed, enabling you to move forward into marriage with a sense of closure, appreciation, and readiness for the new experiences which lie ahead.

- *Good fit for: individual private moment*
- *Children or extended family participation: Not Suitable*
- *Complexity: Easy*

10. Thrive Ritual

Purpose: To connect with the natural world and fairy energies, setting intentions for a loving, harmonious, and prosperous marriage in which you can thrive as an individual.

Materials:

- An outdoor space, preferably in a natural setting like a garden, forest, or near a tree.
- A central candle to symbolize your intentions and connection to the union.
- Natural offerings (such as flowers, berries, or herbs) to honor the fairy realm and nature spirits.
- 2 cups of strong tea.
- A small stone or crystal to symbolize your commitment to a harmonious marriage.

- Incense or essential oils for a sacred atmosphere (optional).
- A small bell or chime.

Preparation:
Choose a serene outdoor location where you feel connected to nature and can be undisturbed. Arrange the central candle in a small clearing or on a natural surface like a rock or tree stump. Place the natural offerings around the candle as a gesture of goodwill to the nature and fairy spirits.

Ritual Steps:

1. Creating a Sacred Space: Begin by ringing the bell or chime softly, inviting positive energy and the presence of nature and fairy spirits. Invite the fae to your sacred space, "I invite the good folk of the land to join me for tea."
2. Lighting the Candle: Light the central candle, focusing on your intentions for a harmonious and loving marriage.
3. Connecting with Nature and Fairy Energy: Take a moment to feel the energy of the natural surroundings. Acknowledge the presence of nature spirits and fairies, asking for their blessings and guidance for your marriage. Place your hands on the ground or touch the bark of a tree, feeling your connection to the earth and its energies.
4. Drink your tea and pour a cup of tea on the ground as an offering of communion with the fairies.
5. Intention Setting with Stone or Crystal: Hold the stone or crystal and silently set your intentions for your future marriage. Focus on harmony, love,

understanding, and personal growth. Place the stone near the base of the central candle, symbolizing the grounding and strengthening of your intentions through nature's energy.

6. Visualization and Fairy Blessing: Close your eyes and visualize your future marriage. Imagine scenes of joy, support, and shared growth, surrounded by the vibrant energy of nature. See yourself thriving as an individual within the marriage. Ask the fairy realm to bless your future union with joy, lightness, and the magic of love. Ask for their assistance in helping you thrive as an individual.

7. Offering Gratitude: Express your gratitude to nature, the fairies, and the spirits for their presence and blessings. Leave the natural offerings as a token of thanks and respect.

8. Closing the Ritual: Extinguish the central candle. Ring the bell or chime again to signify the end of the ritual and to thank the spirits for their guidance and tell the fae your tea time has come to an end.

9. Post-Ritual Reflection: Spend some time in nature, absorbing the tranquility and positive energy. Reflect on the intentions you've set and how you can nurture them in your daily life. In the days leading to your handfasting, revisit the natural site if possible, or simply spend time outdoors to reconnect with the intentions and energies from the ritual.

Through connection with nature and fairy energies, this ritual focuses on the individual's journey towards a harmonious and fulfilling marriage.

- *Good fit for: individual private moment, bridal shower, bachelorette party or bachelor party*
- *Children or extended family participation: could get help from or involve your wedding party participants*
- *Complexity: Easy - Medium*

CHAPTER 7 NON-TRADITIONAL RITUALS FOR COUPLES

Incorporating non-traditional rituals into a handfasting ceremony can complement and enhance traditional elements in several ways:

- Non-traditional rituals can be highly personalized, reflecting your unique personalities, experiences, and values. This personal touch can make traditional elements more meaningful by providing a contemporary context or personal connection. Unique or non-traditional rituals can serve as powerful symbols for the couple's hopes, dreams, and intentions for their marriage, adding another layer of symbolism to the traditional aspects of the ceremony.
- Incorporating non-traditional elements allows for creative expression and innovation in the ceremony. This can make the event more memorable and engaging for the couple and their guests.
- Combining traditional and non-traditional elements creates a balance between honoring heritage and

embracing modernity. This blend can symbolize the joining of past and present, reflecting the journey of the couple and their families.

Rituals for Couples

I designed these next ten non-traditional rituals to provide couples with more options to enhance your handfasting ceremony and pre- and post- handfasting events. By incorporating personalized rituals, a handfasting ceremony becomes more than just a formal event. The ceremony becomes a deeply personal, meaningful, and transformative experience, which truly reflects the essence of the couple's bond. Here are ten examples of rituals for couples:

The List:

11. Abundance
12. Fertility
13. Bond Strengthening
14. Protection
15. Sex Magic
16. Divination for Insights
17. Honeymoon Blessings
18. House Blessing and Clearing
19. Limitless Life Manifestation Box
20. Balance of Divine Feminine/Divine Masculine

11. Abundance

Purpose: To jointly set powerful intentions for abundance in all aspects of their married life – love, health, happiness, and prosperity.

Materials:
- A green candle (for prosperity and abundance)
- A rose quartz crystal (for love and harmony)
- Citrine crystal (for prosperity and positivity)
- A small pot of soil and seeds (symbolizing growth and the nurturing of intentions)
- Two small pieces of paper and pens
- A bowl or small cauldron
- Incense or essential oils (such as cinnamon, orange, or patchouli for abundance)

Preparation: Choose a serene outdoor location where you both feel at peace, preferably surrounded by nature. Set up a small altar or space with the candle, crystals, pot of soil and seeds, paper and pens, and the bowl or cauldron.

Ritual Steps:
1. Creating Sacred Space: Begin by lighting the incense or diffusing the essential oils to cleanse the area and attract positive energy. - Light the green candle together, symbolizing the start of the ritual and your joint intentions for abundance. Smile and think of 3 things you are currently grateful for, basking in the attitude of gratitude in order to raise your vibration.
2. Setting Intentions for Abundance: Sit facing each other with the candle between you. Hold the rose quartz and citrine, one in each hand, and share your individual wishes for abundance in your marriage – this could include emotional richness, financial stability, health, joy, or any other forms of abundance you wish to attract.

3. Writing Down Intentions: Each partner writes their intentions for abundant married life on a piece of paper. Be specific about what you wish to manifest together.

4. Planting Seeds of Intentions: Place the papers at the bottom of the pot. Fill the pot with soil and plant the seeds together. As you plant, visualize your intentions taking root and growing, just as the seeds will grow into plants. Water the seeds, symbolizing the nurturing of your intentions.

5. Affirmations of Abundance: Together, recite affirmations resonating with the theme of abundance. For example, "Together, we attract joy, health, love, and prosperity in our journey. Our marriage is a vessel for abundant blessings."

6. Meditative Reflection: Spend a few moments in meditation, focusing on the candle's flame. Visualize your life together filled with the abundance you have set intentions for, feeling the emotions that this future brings.

7. Sealing the Ritual: Extinguish the candle together, signifying the sealing and sending off of your intentions to the universe. Close the ritual by expressing gratitude to each other for the shared vision and to the universe for its endless abundance.

8. Post-Ritual Practice: Place the pot with the planted seeds in a spot where you can both tend to it regularly, as a reminder of your growing intentions. Keep the crystals in a special place where you can see them often, as a reminder of your commitment to foster abundance in your marriage. In the days leading up to your handfasting, revisit your

intentions and continue to nurture the seeds you planted, both physically and metaphorically.

This ritual not only sets the stage for a marriage filled with abundance but also strengthens the bond between partners as they actively participate in manifesting their shared dreams and aspirations. This one was designed for the couple. The ritual could be tailored for a larger group of participants. I did write another one designed for a group - see # 23.

- *Good fit for: couple private moment, engagement party, rehearsal dinner, reception, honeymoon, house blessing*
- *Children or extended family participation: Could be tailored to include children, family members or wedding party participants*
- *Complexity: Easy*

12. Fertility

Purpose: To harness natural energies and symbolic actions to attract fertility and the blossoming of new life into the marriage.

Materials:
- A natural outdoor setting with access to earth (such as a garden or a quiet spot in a park)
- A shared piece of fruit (symbolizing fertility and abundance)
- Two small to medium sized stones
- Outdoor altar if available
- Two hand fans (paper or fabric)

Preparation: Choose a quiet time to perform the ritual in a natural outdoor setting, which feels peaceful and vibrant.Set up a simple outdoor altar, which could consists of natural material such as a flat rock or tree stump or a man-made cement block

Ritual Steps:
1. Connect with Nature: Begin by spending a few moments connecting with the natural surroundings. Breathe deeply, feeling the energy of the earth, the air, and the life around you.
2. Fruit Sharing Ceremony: Share a piece of fruit together, each taking turns to feed the other. As you eat, contemplate fertility, the sweetness of life, and the abundance that you wish to cultivate in your marriage.
3. Stone or Crystal Exchange: Hold the fertility-associated stones. Charge them with your intentions for fertility and a harmonious marriage. Exchange the stones or crystals, symbolizing the sharing and harmonizing of your individual energies towards a common goal.
4. Meditative Reflection: Stand or sit together with your hands bound, closing your eyes. Spend a few moments in silent meditation, visualizing a fertile and joyful future, filled with the love and vibrancy of family life.
5. Fanning: Use your fans for germination and propagation. Place your stones on an outdoor altar. Use the fans to fan the stones in small upward fanning motions with the intention of sprouting or germinating the intention of fertility. Then use the fans to fan the stones in broad, sweeping motions

outward from the stones with the intention of propagating or spreading the growth of the fertility intention. Move your arm as if you are causing seeds to spread outwards and grow upwards.

6. Closing the Ritual: Conclude the ritual by expressing gratitude to each other for the shared commitment to this journey, and to nature for its blessings and inspiration.

7. Post-Ritual: In the days leading up to your handfasting, continue to nurture the plants as a symbol of your commitment to nurturing each other and any future family.

This ritual is designed to create a deep connection with natural fertility, harmonizing the couple's energies and intentions towards creating new life and fostering growth within their marriage. This one was designed for the couple. The ritual could be tailored for a larger group of participants. I did write another one designed for a group - see # 24.

- *Good fit for: couple private moment, engagement party, reception, honeymoon, house blessing*
- *Children or extended family participation: Could be tailored to include children, family members or wedding party participants*
- *Complexity: Easy*

13. Bond Strengthening

Purpose: To actively engage in practices which enhance and affirm the spiritual and emotional bond between the bride and groom.

Materials:
- A quiet and spacious outdoor area, such as a garden, beach, or forest clearing
- Comfortable clothing suitable for movement
- Two small crystals or stones, ideally ones that are meaningful to both partners (e.g., rose quartz for love, or clear quartz for clarity)
- A blindfold (optional)

Preparation: Choose a peaceful time to perform the ritual in a natural setting, which is private and serene. Keep the crystals or stones in your pockets or a safe place nearby.

Ritual Steps:
1. Grounding and Centering: Begin by standing facing each other, feet firmly planted on the ground. Close your eyes and take deep, synchronized breaths. Feel the earth beneath your feet and the air around you, centering yourselves in the present moment.
2. Synchronized Movement: Start a series of synchronized movements, such as gentle stretching or yoga poses, maintaining eye contact as much as possible. Move slowly and intentionally, mirroring each other's movements to create a sense of unity and harmony.
3. Breathwork for Connection: Stand close, facing each other, and place your hands on each other's heart. Practice synchronized breathing, inhaling and exhaling together. Feel the rhythm of each other's breath and heartbeat, aligning your energies.

4. Guided Blindfold Walk (Optional): One partner wears the blindfold while the other guides them through the natural space. This exercise builds trust and deepens the sense of connection. After a short time, switch roles.

5. Energy Exchange with Stones: Sit facing each other and hold your respective crystals or stones. Share why you chose these particular stones and what they symbolize for your relationship. Exchange the stones and hold the one given by your partner. Feel the energy and intention imbued within it, recognizing the bond it represents.

6. Shared Visualization: Still holding the stones, close your eyes and engage in a shared visualization. Imagine your future together, filled with love, understanding, and mutual support. Visualize overcoming challenges and sharing joyous moments. Build your story together by taking turns expressing parts of your envisioned future.

7. Active Affirmation of Commitment: Stand and face each other again, affirming your commitment aloud. This could be simple statements like, "I commit to our journey with love and trust," or more personalized affirmations of your bond.

8. Concluding the Ritual: Conclude the ritual by embracing, acknowledging the strength and depth of your connection. Express gratitude to each other for the shared experience and to nature for providing a serene setting.

9. Post-Ritual:- Keep the exchanged stones as a reminder of the ritual and your deepened bond. Carry them with you or place them in a special space where they can be seen regularly.

This ritual uses active engagement, breathwork, and movement to foster a deeper understanding and connection, preparing the couple for a spiritually aligned and strong union in their forthcoming handfasting and marriage.

- *Good fit for: couple private moment, engagement party, rehearsal dinner, reception*
- *Children or extended family participation: Could be tailored to include children or family members*
- *Complexity: Easy*

14. Protection

Purpose: To create a protective barrier and bless their upcoming marriage and future family life with safety and security.

Materials:
- Sea salt (about a cup)
- Optional: Crushed eggshells (3 clean shells crushed)
- A small pouch or container
- Paper and a pen (for drawing sigils)
- Optional: Essential oils for cleansing and protection (such as sage, rosemary, or lavender)
- Optional: tablecloth

Preparation: Choose a peaceful area in your home where you both feel comfortable and safe. Prepare the space by clearing any clutter and optionally diffusing essential oils for cleansing. Lay down a tablecloth to sit on to ensure easy cleanup.

Ritual Steps:
1. Creating Protective Sigils: Sit down together and spend a few moments in quiet contemplation of what protection means for your future family. A sigil is a symbol representing an intention. Using the paper and pen, each partner draws a sigil representing protection, safety, and security for your family. Focus on your intention while drawing.
2. Charging the Sigils: Once you have drawn your sigils, hold them between your hands and visualize a protective light enveloping them. Imagine this light charging the sigils with powerful energy.
3. Salt Barrier Creation: Mix sea salt and crushed eggshells together to form a protection powder. Use the protection powder to create a small circle around you as you sit. As you sprinkle the protection powder, envision it forming a protective barrier safeguarding you and your future family from harm.
4. Sigil and Salt Union: Place the charged sigils in the center of the circle. Sprinkle a pinch of protection powder on them, affirming your intention of protection. Say something like, "With these sigils and this salt, we create a shield of protection around our family."
5. Sealing the Sigils: Carefully fold the sigils and place them in the pouch or container with a pinch of protection powder. This container is a talisman of protection for your home and family. Optionally, you can add a few drops of the essential oil to the pouch for additional cleansing and protective properties.
6. Activating the Protection: Holding the pouch together, speak out your intentions and wishes for a safe, secure, and harmonious family life. You can say

something like, "We invoke protection, safety, and peace for our family, now and always."

7. Closing the Ritual: Conclude the ritual by placing the pouch in a prominent place in your home, such as by the front door or in your bedroom. - Express gratitude for the protection and safety granted to your future family.

8. Post-Ritual: In the days leading up to your handfasting, acknowledge the presence of the protective talisman in your home, reinforcing the intention of safety and security for your future together.

This ritual is a powerful way to set a foundation of protection for the couple's married life, using the combined energies of salt and personalized sigils to create a lasting symbol of safety for their family.

- *Good fit for: couple private moment, engagement party, rehearsal dinner, reception, honeymoon, house blessing*
- *Children or extended family participation: Could be tailored to include children or family members*
- *Complexity: Easy*

15. Sex Magic

Purpose: To transform the couple into a power couple to easily attract and manifest their desires through a process of awakening and harmonizing Kundalini energy within each individual, enhancing emotional and spiritual connection in preparation for their handfasting.

Materials:
- A peaceful and private space with a bed or couch
- Ambient, passionate or erotic music for relaxation
- Two crystals such as red jasper or serpentine, associated with the root chakra and Kundalini awakening

Preparation: Create a private and comfortable space where you won't be disturbed. This is best performed without clothing to ensure a sensory experience.

Ritual Steps:
1. Setting the Intention: Sit facing each other with your spines straight, legs crossed if comfortable. Hold your respective crystals and close your eyes. Set a mutual intention to awaken and balance your Kundalini energies in harmony with each other, fostering a deeper spiritual and emotional bond.
2. Breathing and Grounding: Begin with deep, synchronized breathing. As you inhale and exhale, visualize grounding energy connecting you to the earth. This helps in stabilizing your energy before awakening Kundalini.
3. Activating Root Chakra: Focus on your root chakra at the base of your spine, where Kundalini energy resides. Visualize the crystal's energy activating this chakra. Imagine a red light glowing brightly at the base of your spine, representing the energy becoming ready to rise.
4. Visualization of Kundalini Awakening: Envision the Kundalini energy as a coiled serpent at the base of your spine. With each breath, visualize it slowly uncoiling and rising up through your spine. Feel the

energy move through each chakra, clearing and energizing them as it rises.

5. Connecting Kundalini Energy: Connect physically in a comfortable and gentle act of sexual intercourse and move rhythmically together while still picturing the energy surging through your chakras. Once you visualize the Kundalini energy reaching the crown chakra, imagine a beam of light connecting your energies above your heads. This light represents the unity and harmony of your awakened energies. Keep this visualization for a few minutes, feeling the interconnected flow of energy until a climax is achieved.

6. Joint Affirmation: Together, affirm this connection and awakening. You might say, "Together, we awaken and harmonize our energies, strengthening our synergy and power as a couple."

7. Gentle Return: When you feel the process is complete, visualize the energy settling, returning to the root chakra. Take some grounding breaths, bringing your awareness back to the present.

8. Closing the Ritual: Share your experiences and feelings from the ritual, expressing gratitude for the strengthened connection. Place the crystals in a place of importance as a reminder of this shared spiritual journey.

9. Post-Ritual: In the days leading to your handfasting, reflect on this experience. Continue practices nurturing your spiritual connection, such as meditation, yoga, or spending time in nature.

This ritual helps in aligning and harmonizing the couple's energies, creating a profound bond at both a spiritual and emotional level, and setting a strong, unified foundation and projection of couple power for their marriage.

- *Good fit for: couple private moment, upon engagement, honeymoon, throughout marriage*
- *Children or extended family participation: Not Suitable*
- *Complexity: Medium – Advanced*

16. Divination for Insights

Purpose: To gain insights and guidance for the upcoming marriage through a shared Tarot or Oracle card reading.

Materials:
- An Oracle card deck
- A cloth or surface to lay out the cards
- A notebook and pen for taking notes (optional)

Preparation: Choose a time and place where both of you feel relaxed and free from distractions. Set up the space with the card deck, cloth, notebook, and pen.

Ritual Steps:
1. Setting the Intention: Sit together with the card deck. Take a few deep breaths to center yourselves. Holding the deck together, set the intention to receive clear and helpful guidance for your marriage. Invite in helping spirits if desired.
2. Shuffling the Cards: Shuffle the cards together, focusing on your questions and intentions regarding your upcoming marriage. These might include aspects like challenges you might face, strengths you can draw upon, and how you can support each other.

3. Drawing the Cards: Decide on a spread suiting your intention. A simple three-card spread can be sufficient, representing: (1) The foundation of your marriage, (2) Potential challenges, and (3) The strengths or blessings you'll share. Optionally, each partner draws an additional card representing what unique gift they bring to the marriage.   Take turns drawing the cards and laying them out in the chosen spread.

4. Interpreting the Cards: Together, interpret each card and its position in the spread. Discuss what the imagery, symbols, and traditional meanings of the cards might suggest about your future marriage. Be open to each other's perspectives and insights. The discussion itself can be revealing and deepen your understanding of each other.

5. Reflecting and Discussing: Reflect on the overall message of the reading. How do the cards speak to your current situation, hopes, and concerns about your marriage? Discuss how you can use this insight to strengthen your relationship and prepare for your life together.

6. Recording the Reading: If desired, take notes on the reading in the notebook. This can be a helpful reference to look back on as you navigate your marriage.

7. Closing the Ritual: Thank the Tarot or Oracle deck and any helping spirits for the guidance. Share a moment of gratitude with each other for the insights gained and the journey ahead.

8. Post-Ritual: In the days leading up to your handfasting, revisit the insights from the reading.

Consider any actions or discussions you might want to have based on the guidance received.

This ritual is a meaningful way to engage with the spiritual tool of Oracle cards, fostering a deeper understanding and connection as you both prepare to enter into marriage. This one was designed for couples. The ritual could be tailored for a larger group of participants. I did write another one designed for a group - see # 25.

- *Good fit for: couple private moment, engagement party, rehearsal dinner, reception, honeymoon, house blessing*
- *Children or extended family participation: Could be tailored to include children or family members*
- *Complexity: Easy – Medium*

17. Honeymoon Blessing

Building a despacho prayer bundle is a beautiful and symbolic ritual, which can be performed on a honeymoon to bless the couple's future life together. This ritual, rooted in Andean traditions, involves creating a bundle with various natural and symbolic elements, each layer representing different aspects of the couple's future, which is then offered to a fire as a symbol of sending their prayers and intentions to the universe.

Purpose: To offer blessings and intentions for the future of the marriage through the creation and offering of a despacho prayer bundle.

Materials:
- A variety of natural and symbolic items (such as leaves, flowers, seeds, grains, dry beans, sweets, woolen or cloth figures, or small written notes of intentions)
- A pack of tissue paper (can be colored paper used for gift bags, needs to be at least that size)
- String, yarn or ribbon to tie the bundle
- A safe outdoor space with a fire pit or a designated fire area
- Matches or a lighter

Preparation: Gather your materials and find a quiet, peaceful outdoor space where you can build a fire safely.

Ritual Steps:
1. Setting the Intention: Begin by sitting together and discussing your hopes, dreams, and intentions for your married life. Reflect on the aspects of your relationship that you wish to honor and grow.
2. Creating the Despacho Bundle: Lay out the first piece of tissue paper, which serves as the base of your despacho bundle.   - Start placing your items onto the paper, each element representing different aspects of your future life together. For example: Seeds or grains for growth and abundance, flowers for beauty and harmony in your relationship, sweets for the sweetness of life and joy in your marriage, small notes with written intentions or prayers
3. Building Layers: As you add each item, share why you chose it and what it symbolizes for your future. Layer these items with care between sheets of tissue

paper, infusing the despacho with your love and positive intentions.

4. Closing the Bundle: Once you have added all your items, carefully fold the paper like wrapping a gift to enclose them, creating a neat bundle. You can tie it with a natural string or ribbon if needed.

5. Offering the Despacho to the Fire: Safely light your fire in the fire pit. Once the fire is burning steadily, offer the despacho bundle to the flames. As it burns, imagine your prayers and intentions being released to the universe. Spend a moment watching the fire, reflecting on the symbolic release of your hopes and dreams into the world.

6. Meditation and Reflection: Sit together by the fire, meditating on the flames and the life you will build together. Feel the warmth and energy of the fire, symbolizing the strength and passion of your marriage.

7. Closing the Ritual: As the fire dies down, share a moment of gratitude for each other and for the blessings in your life. Conclude the ritual with an embrace or a shared gesture of love.

8. Post-Ritual: As you continue your honeymoon and return to daily life, keep the spirit of this ritual in your hearts. Remember the intentions and blessings you offered and carry them with you as you navigate your journey together.

This despacho prayer bundle ritual is a powerful way to honor and set intentions for your marriage, connecting you with each other and the natural world, and symbolically sending your prayers for your future into the universe.

While designed for a couple on their honeymoon, it could be tailored for anytime.

- *Good fit for: couple private moment, engagement party, rehearsal dinner, reception, honeymoon, house blessing*
- *Children or extended family participation: Could be tailored to include children or family members*
- *Complexity: Medium*

18. House Blessing and Clearing

Purpose: To bless and energetically cleanse the couple's new home, creating a harmonious and sacred space for their married life.

Materials:
- A small bowl of water
- Essential oils (such as lavender for tranquility, rosemary for protection, or sage for cleansing)
- A drum, rattle or any instrument for creating rhythmic sounds
- Incense or smudging herbs (optional)
- Written prayers or affirmations

Preparation:- Prepare the bowl of water by adding a few drops of your chosen essential oils. Bless the water with your intentions for peace, love, and protection in your home. If using, light the incense or smudging herbs to cleanse the space before starting the ritual.

Ritual Steps:

1. Initial Cleansing: Start at the entrance of your home. Use the incense or smudging herbs to cleanse the doorway, setting the intention to allow only positive energy to enter. Open the windows at least a crack to allow negative energies to escape.

2. Anointing with Blessed Water: Dip your fingers in the bowl of blessed water and flick the water in each room. As you do this, visualize the water droplets carrying your intentions, purifying and blessing the space.

3. Drumming and Sound Cleansing: Move from room to room, using the drum or instrument to create rhythmic sounds. The vibrations help break up any stagnant energy and infuse the space with vitality and joy.

4. Prayers or Affirmations: In each room, recite a prayer or affirmation resonating with the purpose of the space. For example: In the living room: "May this space be filled with love, laughter, and shared memories." In the kitchen: "May nourishment and warmth always be found here." In the bedroom: "May this room be a sanctuary of love and rest."

5. Sealing the Ritual: Once you have moved through all the rooms, close the windows and return to your main living area. Join hands and together express gratitude for the home and the life you will build there. Conclude with a shared affirmation, such as, "This home is cleared and sealed. Our home is a haven of happiness, health, and harmony."

6. Closing Celebration: Celebrate the completion of the ritual with a small celebration, perhaps sharing a meal or a toast in your newly blessed home.

7. Post-Ritual: In the days following the ritual, maintain the sense of peace and sanctity in your home. Keep it clean, orderly, and filled with love, remembering the intentions set during the ritual. Keep a spray bottle of the oil-infused blessed water handy to respritz when needed.

This ritual helps in creating a positive and sacred environment in the couple's new home, fostering a space, which supports their relationship and the life they are building together.   This one was designed for the couple. The ritual could be tailored for a larger group of participants. I did write another one designed for a group - see # 27.

- *Good fit for: couple private moment, house blessing*
- *Children or extended family participation: Could be tailored to include children or family members, wedding party participants, or community*
- *Complexity: Medium*

19. Limitless Life Manifestation Box

Purpose: To release fears and embrace a life of limitless possibilities and success as a united couple.

Materials:
- A small box (like a wooden trinket box or any suitable box).
- Two small figurines or images representing the honey badger and the eagle
- A small fire pit or a safe container to burn paper
- Strips of paper and pens

- A bowl of earth or soil
- Two stones representing strength and vision (like tiger's eye or clear quartz)

Preparation: Prepare the space where you will perform the ritual, ideally a place where you can safely make a small fire. Place the figurines or images of the honey badger and the eagle near the fire pit. Have the small box open and ready to receive items during the ritual.

Ritual Steps:
1. Setting Intentions: Begin by sitting together and discussing your shared visions and intentions for a limitless life together. Focus on what you wish to achieve as a couple.
2. Releasing Fears: Write down any fears or doubts, which might be holding you back from achieving your shared goals on the strips of paper. Be honest and open with each other during this process.
3. Invoking the Honey Badger: Hold the honey badger figurine or image, and together, call upon the spirit of the honey badger to imbue you with fearlessness and resilience. You might say, "Spirit of the courageous honey badger, grant us your fearlessness and strength in the face of challenges."
4. Burning Fears: One by one, read aloud the fears written on the paper, then burn them in the fire pit. As the paper burns, visualize releasing these fears, allowing the flames to transform them into courage and determination. Fill courage fill your solar plexus chakra.
5. Invoking the Eagle: Next, hold the eagle figurine or image. Call upon the spirit of the eagle for vision and

success. Say something like, "Spirit of the eagle, bless us with your clarity and vision to see beyond limitations and soar towards our shared dreams. Allow us to fly high as the eagle and above the peaks of our potential to live a life without limitation. "

6. Planting Stones of Strength and Vision: Place the stones in the bowl of earth or soil, symbolizing the planting of your intentions for a limitless life. As you do this, affirm your commitment to support each other's aspirations and to work together towards success.

7. Storing Intentions in the Box: Place the figurines or images of the honey badger and eagle into the box. Transfer the stones from the soil into the box with a tiny bit of the dirt. This act symbolizes containing and nurturing your shared dreams and intentions.

8. Shared Vision Meditation: Sit together with closed eyes, holding hands, and meditate on your shared future. Visualize achieving your goals, overcoming obstacles, and living a life filled with success and fulfillment.

9. Closing the Ritual: Conclude the ritual by expressing gratitude to the spirits of the honey badger and eagle, and to each other for the shared path ahead. Extinguish the fire safely.

10. Post-Ritual:: End the ritual with a small celebration, such as sharing a special meal, to honor the beginning of your journey towards a limitless life together. Try new or exotic foods or recipes at the meal to represent your commitment to courage in face of the unknown. Keep the manifestation box on your altar or in a special place as a reminder of your commitment to a fearless and successful life together. Regularly revisit

the feelings and intentions set during this ritual to maintain focus and motivation on your journey as a couple.

This ritual is designed to unify the couple's energies, fostering a spirit of joint courage, strength, and success as they embark on their married life together.

- *Good fit for: couple private moment, honeymoon, house blessing*
- *Children or extended family participation: Not Suitable*
- *Complexity: Medium*

20. Balance of Divine Feminine/Divine Masculine

Purpose: To celebrate and balance the divine feminine and masculine energies within each individual and between the couple, using the archetypes of the stag and the doe from the west direction.

Materials:
- A natural outdoor setting near water, such as a lake or a river, preferably facing west
- Two masks or symbols representing a stag and a doe or you could use two stone representing divine masculine and divine feminine aspects.
- Comfortable clothing suitable for movement and possibly getting a little wet
- A small portable speaker to play music (optional)
- Two small containers or cups

Preparation: Choose a serene location by the water, ideally where you can watch the sunset in the west. Set up your space with the stag and doe symbols or masks visible.

Ritual Steps:
1. Invocation of Energies: Stand facing the west, close to the water. Begin by invoking the energies of the stag and the doe. You might say, "We call upon the energies of the divine masculine, as strong and steadfast as the stag, and the divine feminine, as intuitive and nurturing as the doe."
2. Embodying the Stag and Doe: Take turns wearing the masks or holding the symbols of the stag and the doe. Embody these energies: one partner embodies the strength and assertiveness of the stag, while the other embodies the grace and intuition of the doe. Discover the divine masculine and the divine feminine energies in each partner.
3. Dance of Balance: Play some music and engage in a playful dance by the water, each embodying the qualities of the stag and doe. Move in ways that reflect strength, assertiveness, grace, and intuition.
4. Water Ritual: Using the containers or cups, each partner scoops water from the natural source. Pour the water over each other's hands, symbolizing the cleansing and harmonizing of your energies. - As you do this, contemplate the flowing, adaptable nature of water, and how it represents the balance of energies within and between you.
5. Affirmation of Balance: Together, affirm your commitment to maintaining balance. You might say, "Together, we honor and balance our divine

masculine and feminine energies, bringing strength, intuition, harmony, and love to our union."

6. Sunset Reflection: As the sun sets in the west, reflect on the union of the divine masculine and feminine within yourselves and in your relationship. Share insights or feelings that arose during the dance and water ritual.

7. Closing the Ritual: As the ritual concludes, express gratitude to the elements, the stag and doe energies, and to each other for this shared experience.

8. Celebratory Moment: Conclude with a light-hearted and celebratory moment, such as skimming stones, taking a dip, or simply enjoying the beauty of the setting.

9. Post-Ritual: Keep the symbols or masks of the stag and doe in your home as reminders of the balance of energies you share. Place near your bed to encourage dreams of divine masculine and divine feminine energies in balance. Regularly engage in activities or practices that honor and nurture both the divine feminine and masculine within yourselves and in your relationship.

This ritual offers a playful yet profound way to acknowledge and harmonize the divine feminine and masculine energies, fostering a balanced and enriched partnership.

- *Good fit for: couple private moment, honeymoon*
- *Children or extended family participation: Not Suitable*
- *Complexity: Easy*

CHAPTER 8 NON-TRADITIONAL RITUALS FOR GROUPS

Rituals for Groups

Group rituals foster a sense of community and belonging among attendees. Participants feel more connected to the ceremony and to each other, which can create a more inclusive and warm atmosphere. hen guests are involved in rituals, it symbolizes their support and unity with the couple. This can be especially meaningful in handfasting ceremonies, which often emphasize the importance of community and collective blessings. Being actively involved in a ceremony makes it more memorable for guests. They're likely to remember how they felt being part of the couple's special day, rather than merely observers.

The follow ten non-traditional rituals for groups
are intended for those looking for non-traditional options for the various events associated with handfasting.

The List:

21. Cacao Community Ritual
22. Fire Blessings
23. Seed or Tree Planting for Abundance
24. Fertility Ritual
25. Group Divination
26. Love Dance
27. Home Blessing Rite
28. Land Healing Rite
29. Gratitude Ritual
30. Community Blessing Ritual

21. Cacao Community Ritual

Purpose: To celebrate and create a heartfelt connection among the inner circle wedding party, raising the group's vibration and strengthening their bonds in support of the couple's journey.

Materials:
- High-quality ceremonial cacao (either in a block or powder form)
- Water or milk
- A large pot and a heat source for preparing the cacao drink
- Cups for serving the cacao
- Comfortable seating arranged in a circle
- Soothing and uplifting background music
- Optional: Flowers, crystals, or other natural elements for creating a sacred space
- A talking stick or a special object to pass around for speaking

Preparation: Prepare the space where the ceremony will be held, arranging seats in a circle and setting a calm, welcoming atmosphere with music and decorations. Brew the ceremonial cacao. Heat water or milk in a large pot and gradually add the cacao, stirring continuously. The cacao should be rich and smooth.

Ritual Steps:
1. Opening the Ceremony: Gather everyone in the circle and welcome them to the cacao ceremony. Explain the purpose of the ceremony: to celebrate the upcoming handfasting, raise the group's vibration, and strengthen the bonds within the party.
2. Setting Intentions: Invite each participant to set a personal intention for the ceremony, focusing on openness, love, and support for the couple and each other.
3. Blessing the Cacao: Before serving the cacao, lead the group in a short blessing. Thank the cacao spirit for its heart-opening qualities and ask for its support in deepening the connections within the group.
4. Serving the Cacao: Serve the cacao to each person in the circle. As they receive their cup, encourage them to feel the warmth and to hold it near their heart for a moment. You can ask the participants to drink their cacao all at the same time or to sip it informally as they are led.
5. Sharing Circle: Begin a sharing circle using the talking stick or special object. Pass it around the circle, allowing each person to share their thoughts, feelings, or blessings for the couple. This can include stories, wishes, poems, or songs.

6. Group Affirmation: After everyone has shared, lead the group in a collective affirmation or chant resonating with the theme of unity and support. For instance, "Together, we support [Bride's Name] and [Groom's Name], united in love and joy."

7. Raising the Vibration: Conclude the sharing portion with a fun and uplifting activity. This could be a group dance, a song, or a laughter yoga session – anything raising the group's energy and joy.

8. Closing the Ceremony: Close the ceremony by expressing gratitude to the cacao spirit, to each participant, and to the couple. End with a group hug or a collective cheer for the couple's future happiness.

9. Post-Ceremony: Continue the celebration with music, dancing, or any other festive activities planned for the event. Encourage the wedding party to carry the positive energy and heartfelt connections from the cacao ceremony into the handfasting ceremony and beyond.

A cacao ceremony is a beautiful way to create a shared, heart-centered experience. It's perfect for fostering deep connections and joy among friends and family as they celebrate and support the couple's journey into marriage.

- *Good fit for:* small groups such as an engagement party, bridal shower, bachelor or bachelorette party, or rehearsal dinner or an impromptu gathering of the inner circle wedding party
- *Children or extended family participation: Suitable*
- *Complexity: Easy*

22. Fire Blessings

Purpose: To strengthen the bond and teamwork among the wedding party members through a joyful and energetic fire ritual, fostering a sense of unity and celebration.

Materials:
- A safe outdoor space with a fire pit
- Firewood and materials to safely start and maintain a fire
- Drums or percussion instruments for each participant (optional)
- Comfortable clothing suitable for movement

Preparation: Set up the fire pit, ensuring all safety measures are in place. If using drums or percussion instruments, have them ready around the fire pit. Arrange a clear space around the fire pit for movement and dancing.

Ritual Steps:
1. Lighting the Fire: Begin the ritual by lighting the fire together. As the fire ignites, encourage everyone to focus on the warmth and light, symbolizing the energy and joy of the group.
2. Circle of Unity: Once the fire is burning steadily, invite everyone to form a circle around it, holding hands. This circle represents unity, support, and the collective strength of the group.
3. Rhythmic Movement: Start a simple side-to-side step in unison, moving around the fire. Gradually, this can evolve into more playful and energetic movements. It is helpful for one person to lead the group so that others know how long to perform the movements.

Encourage laughter and spontaneous expression. Take precautions to ensure the area is safe to move around the fire without tripping and falling in.

4. Drumming and Percussion: If you have drums or percussion instruments, introduce them into the ritual. Start with a simple, steady rhythm which everyone can follow. Encourage each person to add their unique beat or sound, creating a vibrant and harmonious collective rhythm and encourage chanting as participants are led to do so.

5. Fire Gazing Meditation: Pause the movement and drumming for a moment of fire gazing. Invite everyone to silently observe the flames, reflecting on the warmth and energy shared in the group.

6. Closing the Circle: Conclude the ritual with a round of gratitude where each person can express their appreciation for the group, the fire, and the shared experience. End the ritual with a cheer or a group shout, releasing any remaining energy into the night sky.

7. Post-Ritual: Enjoy the rest of the evening together, basking in the joy and connection fostered by the ritual.

This fire ritual is a fantastic way for the inner circle to bond and build teamwork in a joyful, energetic, and memorable way. The combination of movement, drumming, and fire creates a powerful shared experience, reinforcing the unity and support essential during the handfasting ceremony and celebrations.

- *Good fit for:* small groups such as an engagement party, bridal shower, bachelor or bachelorette party, or rehearsal dinner or an impromptu gathering of the inner circle wedding party

- *Children or extended family participation: Suitable*
- *Complexity: Easy-Medium*

23. Seed or Tree Planting for Abundance

Purpose: To celebrate the union of the couple and bestow blessings of fertility, while simultaneously honoring and giving back to the Earth.

Materials:

- Tree saplings or seed packets appropriate for the local climate and ecosystem
- Gardening tools (like spades or trowels)
- Watering cans or a source of water
- A chosen outdoor planting location (ensure permissions if required)
- Biodegradable labels and pens (optional to mark who planted each sapling or seeds)

Preparation: Choose a suitable outdoor location for planting, such as a garden, park, or a specially designated area, which could benefit from more trees. You must have permission from the landowner unless it takes place on your own land. Prepare the saplings or seeds, along with the necessary tools and water.

Ritual Steps:

1. Opening Words: Gather the wedding party at the planting site. Begin with a few words about the significance of the ritual: celebrating the couple's union, wishing them fertility and joy, and giving back

to the Earth. Call upon Gaia or Pachamama to reside over the ritual.

2. Blessing the Saplings or Seeds: Hold the saplings or seeds together and invite everyone to place their hands near them (without touching). Together, say a blessing or express intentions for the couple's fruitful future and the health of the planet. For example, "May these saplings (or seeds) grow strong and resilient, just like [Couple's Names]'s love, bringing beauty and life to our Earth."

3. Planting Process: Guide the wedding party to start planting the saplings or seeds. Each person can take turns doing the actual planting, or work in small teams if there are many participants. If using labels, let each person write their name or a short blessing for the couple and the Earth on a label and place it near their sapling or seed patch.

4. Watering the Plants: Once all the saplings or seeds are planted, everyone takes turns to water them. This act symbolizes the nurturing and support the community offers to the couple and the newly planted life.

5. Circle of Reflection: After planting, form a circle around the planted area. Reflect on the growth that lies ahead - both for the plants and for the couple's relationship. Share a moment of silence to absorb the significance of what was done.

6. Closing the Ritual: End the ritual with a shared affirmation or a cheer, celebrating the couple's future and the contribution to the Earth. Optionally, the couple can express their gratitude to the wedding party for participating in this meaningful act.

7. Post-Ritual: Take photos of the group with the newly planted saplings or seed area as a keepsake.

Encourage the wedding party to revisit the site in the future to see the growth and changes, symbolizing the enduring nature of the couple's love and the lasting impact of their union.

This ritual not only adds a meaningful and eco-friendly element to the wedding festivities but also strengthens the bond within the inner circle as they come together to perform a nurturing and life-affirming act. It also integrates the couple into the community.

- *Good fit for: This ritual is suited for the inner circle and/or the handfasting event guests and can be performed before the wedding at the engagement party or other pre-handfasting event or it can be performed at the reception following the handfasting and involve everyone present. The couple should provide the materials.*
- *Children or extended family participation: Suitable*
- *Complexity: Medium – Advanced*

24. Fertility Ritual

Purpose: To unite the guests in a collective act of celebration and blessings for the couple's fertility and prosperous future together.

Materials:
- A small pouch of flower petals or seeds (such as lavender or chamomile for relaxation and love, or seeds symbolizing growth and fertility)
- A central focal point, like a designated tree, a large pot with soil, or a decorative bowl
- Soft, celebratory background music

Preparation: Distribute small pouches of flower petals or seeds to each guest upon their arrival at the reception or set them out on tables. Prepare the central focal point where the petals or seeds will be offered.

Ritual Steps:
1. Ritual Announcement: At an appropriate moment during the reception, have the officiant or a designated person announce the commencement of the group ritual. Briefly explain the purpose and significance of the ritual to the guests.
2. Gathering Around the Focal Point: Invite all guests to gather around the central focal point. This could be done in a way that doesn't disrupt the flow of the reception too much, such as during a lull in dining or right before a toast.
3. Sharing Fertility Blessings: Begin the ritual by asking the guests to think of a blessing, wish, or positive thought for the couple's future, focusing specifically on fertility and abundance.
4. Offering Petals or Seeds: On a given signal (such as a soft chime or a specific cue in the music), invite each guest to come forward and sprinkle or place their petals or seeds into the tree, pot, or bowl. As they make their offering, they can silently or softly say their blessing for the couple.
5. Group Affirmation: Once all guests have made their offering, lead them in a simple group affirmation. This could be a repeated phrase, such as "Together, we bless and celebrate [Couple's Names]'s journey in love and life."

6. Celebratory Applause or Cheer: Conclude the ritual with a round of applause or a collective cheer, celebrating the couple and the shared hopes for their future.
7. Continuing the Reception: Transition smoothly back into the reception activities, carrying the positive energy from the ritual into the rest of the celebration.
8. Post-Ritual: The couple can keep the tree, planted pot, or decorative bowl with petals and seeds as a keepsake of the blessings received from their loved ones.

This group ritual not only involves the guests in a meaningful way but also strengthens the sense of community and shared joy in the celebration of the couple's union. This may be a good alternative to throwing birdseed, lavender or other traditional bits at the couple after the wedding, especially at venues, which do not allow tossing items due to the mess.

- *Good fit for: reception, house blessing*
- *Children or extended family participation: Suitable*
- *Complexity: Easy*

25. Group Divination

Purpose: To gather close friends and family for a lighthearted yet insightful divination session, aiming to foresee and share blessings for the couple's future.

Materials:
- A deck of Tarot or Oracle cards (easy-to-understand decks are preferable for a wider appeal)

- Comfortable seating arranged in a circle
- A small table or central area to lay out cards
- Optional: Light refreshments and a relaxing ambiance with soft music or ambient lighting

Preparation: Create a comfortable space where the group can sit together. Arrange the seating in a circle with the table in the center. If using, set up the ambiance with soft music or lighting.

Ritual Steps:
1. Opening the Circle: Begin by having everyone sit in a circle. Introduce the purpose of the ritual – to use divination as a way to bring forth positive insights and blessings for the couple's future.
2. Grounding and Focusing: Encourage the group to take a few deep breaths together to center and focus their energies. This step helps to create a harmonious and connected group dynamic.
3. Shuffling the Cards: Pass the Tarot or Oracle deck around the circle, allowing each participant to shuffle the cards while thinking of the couple and their future.
4. Drawing Cards: Once the deck has made a full round, invite each participant to draw a card (or a few cards, depending on the size of the group) from the deck. Go around the circle and have each person reveal their card(s) to the group.
5. Sharing Insights: Each participant interprets the card they drew, focusing on positive and uplifting messages. Encourage creativity and intuition in the interpretations – they don't have to be traditional Tarot meanings. The interpretations can be in the

form of blessings, well-wishes, or predictions of joyful events and experiences in the couple's future.

6. Group Reflection: After everyone has shared, open the floor for a brief group reflection. Discuss any common themes or particularly poignant messages that came up.

7. Closing the Circle: Conclude the ritual by thanking everyone for their insights and participation. Share a toast or a cheer for the couple's happy and blessed future.

8. Post Ritual Transition into the next part of the bachelor or bachelorette party or inner circle gathering, carrying the positive energy forward. The couple can be told about the general themes or specific blessings that came up during the ritual as a fun and heartwarming insight into their friends' and family's wishes for them.

This group divination ritual is not only a fun activity for a gathering but also a meaningful way to involve the couple's loved ones in envisioning and blessing their shared future.

- *Good fit for:* This is good fit for a small group or at the bachelor or bachelorette party
- *Children or extended family participation: Suitable*
- *Complexity: Easy – Medium*

26. Love Dance

Purpose: To unite all guests in a joyful dance which symbolically invokes a spirit of love, harmony, and celebration at the reception and bestow blessings of love on the couple.

Materials:
- An open space for dancing
- A selection of music which is uplifting and easy to dance to
- Optional: Handheld ribbons or small bells for guests to use during the dance

Preparation: Ensure there's enough space at the reception venue for a group dance. Choose a selection of songs that are universally appealing and easy to move to. Consider including a mix of slow and faster-paced music to accommodate different energy levels and dancing preferences.

Ritual Steps:
1. Announcing the Dance Ritual: Have the DJ, band leader, or a designated person announce the start of the group dance ritual. Explain this dance is a special part of the celebration, aimed at spreading and sharing love among all present. It could take place right after the wedding couple's dance.
2. Gathering on the Dance Floor: Invite all guests to the dance floor. Encourage them to form a large circle around the couple, holding hands if comfortable. The couple in the center should hold hands or clap rhythmically to the music if so inclined.
3. Starting with Slow Music: Begin with a slow, gentle song to allow everyone to sync with the rhythm and feel connected as a group. This part of the dance should be simple and inclusive, with easy side-to-side steps or swaying movements.

4. Raising the Energy: Gradually transition to more upbeat music. Encourage guests to move more freely, releasing inhibitions and celebrating the joy of the occasion. If using ribbons or bells, hand them out to guests to add a playful and festive element to the dance.
5. Leading with Love: Throughout the dance, remind guests (either through the music choice or with gentle prompts from the DJ or band) that each step and movement is a celebration of love – not just for the couple but among all present.
6. Incorporating Symbolic Movements: Include simple, symbolic movements, which everyone can follow, such as raising hands upwards to send love out into the world, or forming smaller circles within the larger group to symbolize unity and connection.
7. Closing the Dance: Conclude the group dance with a final, slower song, allowing the energy to settle. Invite everyone to place a hand over their heart for a moment, feeling the warmth and love generated by the dance.
8. Final Applause and Cheers: End with a round of applause or cheers, celebrating the love and joy shared during the dance.
9. Post-Dance: Transition back to the regular festivities of the reception, carrying the uplifted and loving energy forward.

This group dance ritual is not only a fun and interactive part of the wedding reception but also a meaningful way to create a collective experience of joy, love, and unity among all the guests.

- *Good fit for: This is a good fit for the reception or engagement party for all guests.*
- *Children or extended family participation: Suitable*
- *Complexity: Easy*

27. Home Blessing Rite

Purpose: To bless the couple's home with the positive energy and support of their family and inner circle.

Materials:
- A small bundle of dried sage (for smudging) or incense sticks
- A bell or chimes
- A small bowl of salt (for purity and protection)
- Fresh flowers or a potted plant
- A loaf of bread and a bottle of wine or non-alcoholic beverage
- Light, celebratory music (optional)

Preparation: Arrange for the group to gather in front of the couple's home. Prepare the sage, bell, salt, flowers, bread, and beverage in an easily accessible place.

Ritual Steps:
1. Opening the Ceremony: Begin outside the front of the home. Have the couple express their intention for the ceremony, such as inviting love, harmony, and happiness into their living space.
2. Smudging or Incense Lighting: Light the sage or incense and waft the smoke around the couple and the front doorway. This act is meant to cleanse the

space and the couple, preparing them for a new beginning.

3. Entrance Blessing: Ring the bell or chimes at the front door to symbolize the welcoming of positive energy. Sprinkle a pinch of salt across the threshold for protection and to purify the entrance.

4. Moving to the Main Living Area: Invite everyone to enter the home and gather in the main living area. Place the flowers or plant in a central location as a symbol of life and growth.

5. Group Blessing: Once everyone is gathered, invite each person to share a brief blessing or positive wish for the couple and their home. This could be a simple statement or thought.

6. Breaking Bread: Conclude the ceremony by breaking bread together. The couple can start by breaking a piece and sharing it with each other, then passing the loaf around for each guest to break a piece. Pour the wine or beverage and have everyone join in a toast to the couple's happiness and prosperity in their new home.

7. Celebratory Closure: End the ceremony with some celebratory music, allowing everyone to relax and enjoy the moment. This can transition naturally into a casual gathering or reception.

8. Post-Ceremony: The bread and wine/beverage serve as a reminder of the love and unity shared by the group, symbolizing sustenance and joy in the couple's new life together.

This home blessing ceremony creates a warm, inclusive atmosphere, focusing on communal blessings and the simple yet profound act of sharing bread and toasting to the couple's future in their new home.

- *Good fit for: house-warming party, home blessing*
- *Children or extended family participation: It is meant for the family, extended family, and /or inner circle*
- *Complexity: Easy*

28. Land Healing Rite

Purpose: To collectively bless and heal the land surrounding the couple's living space, creating a harmonious connection with nature and contributing to the Earth's well-being.

Materials:
- Natural offerings like seeds, flowers, water, and biodegradable food items (such as fruits or grains)
- A small shovel or trowel
- Several small stones or crystals, charged with intentions of energy
- A bowl of water, preferably from a natural source
- Drums, rattles or flutes, other instruments (optional)

Preparation: Gather the group on the land that is to be blessed and healed. Prepare the offerings and have the shovel, stones or crystals, and bowl of water ready.

Ritual Steps:
1. Opening the Rite: Begin by forming a circle and holding hands. The couple can start the ritual by expressing their intention to bless and heal the land they will be living on. Give an invocation calling on

the spirits of the land and invite them to oversee the ceremony. You may also call in the elements and/or directions.

2. Land Acknowledgment: Acknowledge the land and its history. Recognize its past, present, and future, and express gratitude for its sustenance and beauty.

3. Offering to the Earth: Walk around the land, making natural offerings. Plant seeds as symbols of growth, lay down flowers as symbols of beauty, and scatter biodegradable food as an offering of sustenance, such as milk and oats. - As each offering is made, say a few words of blessing and healing for the land.

4. Crystal and Stone Placement: Place the charged stones or crystals in various spots on the land. These act as anchors for positive energy and intentions. Each person can set a personal intention as they place a stone, focusing on healing, growth, and harmony with nature.

5. Water Blessing: Use the bowl of water to pour water onto the land in a few spots, symbolizing nourishment and purity. You can also invite participants to touch the water and then touch the land, forming a physical connection.

6. Rhythmic Connection: If you have drums or instruments, create a gentle rhythm, which mimics the heartbeat of the Earth. This can help deepen the group's connection to the land and to each other.

7. Silent Reflection: Spend a few moments in silence, allowing everyone to personally connect with the land, sending it healing thoughts and energy.

8. Closing the Ritual: Gather back in the circle. Share a final moment of gratitude for the land, for each other's company, and for the blessings of nature.

Thank and honor the nature spirits of the land that attended. Close the rite with a collective affirmation, such as, "Together, we honor and heal this land, and in turn, are healed and nurtured by it."

9. Post-Ritual: Encourage the participants to continue to nurture and care for the land in practical ways, such as planting native flora, create or maintain habitats for local wildlife, holding regular clean up initiatives or simply spending time appreciating its beauty.

This land healing rite is a meaningful way to deepen the relationship between the couple, their loved ones, and the natural world. It emphasizes the importance of ecological awareness and respect for the Earth, while also setting a foundation of harmony and balance for the couple's life on their land.

- *Good fit for: This can be performed in conjunction with the Home Blessing Rite or done as a separate ceremony.*
- *Children or extended family participation: This is well-suited for family and friends, inner circle wedding party, but can be extended to like-minded neighbors who want to bless the lands of the area where they live.*
- *Complexity: Easy – Medium*

29. Gratitude Ritual

Purpose: To unite guests in a collective expression of gratitude, elevating the group's energy and fostering a sense of harmony and connection. It should only last around 3 minutes and guests can perform seated or standing in front of their chairs.

Preparation: None required.

Ritual Steps:
1. Invitation to Participate: Before the ceremony begins, have the officiant or a designated person briefly explain the purpose of the gratitude ritual and invite all guests to participate.
2. Grounding and Centering: Ask everyone to sit or stand comfortably in front of their chairs. Invite them to close their eyes and take a few deep breaths, centering themselves in the moment.
3. Focusing on Gratitude: Guide the guests to bring to mind something they are grateful for. It could be related to the couple, the beautiful day, their own lives, or anything that evokes a sense of thankfulness.
4. Collective Breath of Gratitude: After a moment of reflection, lead the group in a collective deep breath. As everyone inhales, they should visualize drawing in positivity and gratitude. As they exhale, imagine releasing any stress or negativity.
5. Silent Acknowledgment: In the next breath, encourage each guest to silently acknowledge their gratitude, feeling its warmth in their heart.
6. Shared Vibrational Moment: On the next inhale, invite the guests to hum or make a soft 'ahh' sound as they exhale, creating a gentle, harmonious sound together. This shared vibration serves as a collective expression of gratitude and unity.
7. Closing the Ritual: After the hum, invite the guests to open their eyes and offer a smile or nod to those around them, acknowledging their shared experience. The officiant or designated person can then conclude

the ritual, perhaps saying, "With hearts filled with gratitude, we are now ready to celebrate this union."

8. Post-Ritual: The ceremony can now begin, with the guests feeling more connected and harmoniously aligned.

This gratitude ritual is an effective way to quickly and easily raise the energy of the group, fostering a sense of communal appreciation and connectedness as they prepare to witness the handfasting ceremony.

- *Good fit for: handfasting ceremony (before it begins)*
- *Children or extended family participation: Suitable for all handfasting guests*
- *Complexity: Easy*

30. Community Blessing Ritual

Purpose: To spread blessings and wishes of prosperity from the newlywed couple to their community, enhancing neighborhood bonds and goodwill.

Materials:
- A basket of small, symbolic gifts (such as seeds for growth, small crystals for harmony, friendship bread or bread dough, or handwritten blessings)
- A central gathering area or table
- Light, uplifting background music (optional)

Preparation: Prepare the basket with the small gifts. Set up a central area in the block party where the ritual can take place or instead visit door to door.

Ritual Steps:
1. Opening Announcement: The couple makes a brief announcement to gather the neighbors for the ritual. They can explain the purpose: to share blessings and prosperity with the community.
2. Sharing Symbolic Gifts: The couple begins by taking the basket of gifts and explaining their symbolism (e.g., seeds representing growth and prosperity for the neighborhood). Invite each neighbor to take a gift from the basket as a token of shared blessings and community spirit. If going door to door, take one small gift to each house on the block and leave with a note of blessing.
3. Group Blessing: With everyone gathered, the couple leads a simple group blessing. This could be a short statement like, "Together, we bless our community with harmony, growth, and prosperity. May we all thrive and support each other."
4. Celebratory Closure: Conclude the ritual with a cheer or applause, celebrating the community spirit. Transition back into the block party festivities.
5. Post-Ritual: Whether in a group setting or individual visits, the ritual aims to reinforce the sense of community and to establish the couple as caring and involved members of their neighborhood.

This community blessing ritual by the newlywed couple serves as a meaningful gesture of reaching out and sharing joy and goodwill with their neighbors, whether celebrated together at a community event or through personal interactions. The couple can initiate this ritual for like-minded members of their local community shortly after their marriage. While it does not have to be done at the time of the wedding, it could be connected to a national holiday when the community sometimes gathers and holds block parties (Memorial Day, Halloween, etc.). You may need to send invitations to gather or you could meet with one or two neighbors at a time.

- *Good fit for: reception, house blessing/house warming*
- *Children or extended family participation: Suitable*
- *Complexity: Easy*

In essence, group rituals in handfasting ceremonies not only add a layer of richness and depth to the event but also create a shared experience strengthening the bonds within the community gathered to celebrate the union.

CHAPTER 9 SYMBOLISM AND CUSTOMIZATION

Symbols are the language of the soul. They are the keys that unlock the doors to deeper understanding and connection. In a Pagan wedding, symbols carry a profound meaning, which enhances the sacredness of the union. Let's delve into the rich tapestry of symbolism, which can be woven into your handfasting ceremony and can add customization for your own preferences. Consider what is most important to both of you. Are there spiritual beliefs, cultural traditions, or personal values that you want to honor? If you're drawn to certain cultural or spiritual practices, research the symbols commonly used in those traditions to understand their meanings and appropriateness.

Incorporating Symbolism into Your Handfasting Ceremony

When interweaving symbolism into your handfasting ceremony, you have discretion of how much symbolism to include. Not everything has to be symbolic. Here are some ideas for how you can use symbolism.

Altar setup: Decorate the altar with items holding personal or spiritual significance. This can include crystals for specific energies (like rose quartz for love), candles in colors representing different aspects of your relationship, or figures/statues of deities or symbols resonating with your spiritual beliefs. Use natural elements like stones, leaves, or water to represent the Earth and its elements, reflecting the grounding and life-giving aspects of nature in your union.

Decor and clothing: A representative color theme and symbol can permeate everything from invitations to flowers to tablecloths as well as the clothing of the couple and inner circle participants. Wear attire reflecting your cultural background or personal style. Incorporate symbols into your clothing, like embroidery or jewelry holding a special meaning.

Food: Include symbolic herbs or food choices at the reception or at pre-nuptial events. Use certain symbolic food-based rituals.

Ritual components: Rings, handfasting cords and other rituals tools and elements can be customized to include symbols, colors, gems, or other meaningful items.

Choose colors and materials for the handfasting cord symbolizing aspects of your relationship. For example, red for passion, green for luck, or gold for prosperity. Incorporate charms or beads into the cord holding special meanings, such as heirlooms or tokens from key moments in your relationship.

Choose rings or other items to exchange holding symbolic significance, such as family heirlooms, or custom-made pieces which incorporate symbols or inscriptions that are meaningful to you.

Use specific rituals, which have symbolic meanings, such as lighting a unity candle to symbolize the joining of two lives into one. Incorporate traditional rituals from your cultural background to honor your heritage.

Vows: Include symbolic language in your vows reflecting your beliefs and values. This could involve promising to support each other through specific life stages or challenges, using metaphors which are meaningful to you both.

Customizing Rituals

You can choose a ritual from the lists in Chapters 2-8 and customize further by including symbolism of your choice. Choose colors, flowers, crystals and symbols which hold meaning for you to use in each ritual, whether it is a traditional or non-traditional ritual. See symbolism themes below.

Another way you can customize rituals is by changing various aspects of the ritual - think about the who, what, where, how and why. For illustration, let's analyze the individual ritual 'Release Ritual' from Chapter 6.

Who: This ritual is written for individuals, but I could customize it for a couple instead.

For a couple, the why (purpose), what (materials) and where would not change. However, I might need to change the how. For instance, perhaps the couple agrees to write specific blocks or negative energies they want to release together instead of coming up with individual statements to write. In the burning ceremony, you might change the words from I to we or even add additional statements about the intention or outcome. In the crystal and water for healing step, you may have each partner anoint the other with water and touch them with the crystal. In essence, think about aspect you want to change and how that affects the other aspects.

When customizing a ritual to involve children, consider any risks to safety, which the particular ritual might involve, such as use of fire. Make it fun for them. If the steps are too complex, it could lead to anxiety or a failure to complete it. Don't give children too critical of a role as they can be unpredictable.

I gave my daughter a role in our handfasting ceremony when she was five. She was to be the feather girl. Her job was to carry a basket of feathers and hand them out to the guests on the ends of the aisles as the walked down the aisle. She cried the whole time and did not hand out any feathers. She was scared to be in the spotlight in front of a crowd. She did not understand the step of handing out of the feathers, even though we had gone over it beforehand. I thought she wanted to participate, but when the event actually happened, it did not work out as planned. I felt bad that she was stressed out. Don't worry too much when your plans are not executed as envisioned. It was not critical for my daughter to hand out feathers. Guests thought she was adorable.

Download a free template from my website for building and customizing the handfasting rituals. KatSticker.com/downloads

Symbolism Themes

The symbolism examples below are organized by the meaning of 15 common themes, which couples choose to include in their nuptial events. Beneath each theme, you will find representative colors, flowers, crystals, symbols, representative rituals/events and, where applicable, timing/directions. This is not an all-inclusive list but a sampling of common symbolism. If a different color, flower, crystal, and so forth resonates better with you based on your experiences, beliefs and traditions, by all means incorporate it into your ceremony instead. The symbolism is part of your unique journey to make your sacred union as meaningful as possible. Consider it all mix and match.

1. Abundance / Prosperity

Colors: gold, green, red

Flowers: sunflower, dahlia, peony, iris, alstroemeria

Herbs: turmeric, chamomile, alfalfa, cloves, parsley

Crystals/gems: peridot, carnelian, pyrite, jade, tigers eye

Symbols: acorn, coins/cash, apple, almond, lentils, honey, grapes

Timing/Direction: autumn, west

Rituals/Events: blessings, divination

2. Fertility

Colors: green, pink

Flowers: dandelion, lotus, orchids

Herbs: catnip, black cohosh, red rasberry leaf, evening primrose

Crystals/gems: moonstone, celestite, green adventurine, rose quartz

Symbols: acorn, ankh, dragon, horned god, wedding cake, bees

Timing/Direction: spring, east

Rituals/Events: tossing grain/rice

3. Harmony

Colors: green, indigo, lavender

Flowers: lotus, peace lily, white rose

Herbs: lavender, oregano, maca root

Crystals/gems: selenite, smoky quartz, zebra quartz, malachite, angelite

Symbols: double spiral, yin and yang, dove, flower of life, endless knot, pentacle

Timing/Direction: full moon

Rituals/Events: invocation

4. Health and Healing

Colors: green, blue, white and red

Flowers: magnolia, camelia, lavender

Herbs: marjoram, mint, echinacea, mullein

Crystals/gems: clear quartz, amethyst, rose quartz, jasper, hematite

Symbols: fire, water, hexahedron, tetrahedron, swan, oak tree

Timing/Direction: south, summer, mid-day

Rituals/Events: raise a toast

5. Joy and Happiness

Colors: amber, yellow, pink, lavender

Flowers: yellow lily, yellow rose, lily of the valley, mums

Herbs: St Johns wort, lemon balm, gotu kola

Crystals/gems: amber, citrine, turquoise, sunstone

Symbols: rainbow, dragonfly, sun, fireworks, stars

Rituals/Events: reception celebration

6. Longevity

Colors: grey, copper

Flowers: lotus, peony

Herbs: rosemary, astragalus, goji berry, ginger, sage

Crystals/gems: aquamarine, labradorite, amethyst, jade, bloodstone, river rock

Symbols: pine tree, eye of horus, infinity, ourosbouros, crane, deer, tortoise

Rituals/Events: raise a toast

7. Love and Commitment

Colors: red, pink

Flowers: red and pink roses, tulip

Herbs: cinnamon, hibiscus, jasmine, damiana

Crystals/gems: emerald, ruby, kunzite, rose quartz, malachite

Symbols: infinity, heart, hearts intertwined, trinity, Serch Bythol

Rituals/Events: exchange of rings, tie the knot with handfasting cord

8. Luck

Colors: seafoam green, beige

Flowers: shamrocks, bamboo, peonies, heather

Herbs: basil, lemongrass, mint, aloe

Crystals/gems: turquoise, citrine, green adventurine, amazonite

Symbols: horseshoe, #7

Rituals/Events: carrying a horseshoe

9. New Beginnings / Renewal

Colors: red, pink, yellow

Flowers: sprouts, white spider lily, cherry blossom

Herbs: tea tree, red clover, blessed thistle

Crystals/gems: rainbow moonstone, chrysocolla, opal, blue kyanite

Symbols: Seed of life symbol, phoenix, gourd, pear, maple leaf, scarab

Timing/Direction: spring, east, morning, new moon

Rituals/Events: jumping the broom, sweeping the house

10. Protection

Colors: black, white

Flowers: calendula, marigold, eucalyptus

Herbs: angelica, rue, garlic, sage

Crystals/gems: black tourmaline, smoky quartz, black kyanite

Symbols: Metatron's cube, salt, ash tree, hawthorne tree

Rituals/Events: smudging, invocation/ calling directions

11. Purity / purification

Colors: white

Flowers: calla lily, white rose, daisy, babys breath

Herbs: bay laurel, fennel, hyssop

Crystals/gems: flourite, herkamer diamond, selenite, garnet

Symbols: doves, white wedding gown, cotton

Rituals/Events: ritual bath

12. Romance

Colors: red, pink, orange

Flowers: orange rose, lilac, camellia, bird of paradise

Herbs: patchouli, basil, coriander, ylang ylang

Crystals/gems: pink tourmaline, lapis lazuli, morganite

Symbols: fire, harp, swans, hearts, chocolate, love birds, flowers

Timing/Direction: summer, south

Rituals/Events: dancing, newlywed's kiss

13. Spiritual Connection

Colors: purple, white, silver

Flowers: white lily, lotus, jasmine

Herbs: sandalwood, frankincense, thyme

Crystals/gems: k2, azurite, lepidolite, clear quartz

Symbols: octahedron, #9, spider

Timing/Direction: north, full moon, winter

Rituals/Events: invocation, meditation

14. Union / Unity / Family

Colors: blue, rainbow or multicolored

Flowers: hydrangea, allium, hyacinth

Herbs: yarrow, agrimony, comfrey

Crystals/gems: ruby zoicite, rutilated quartz, tiger iron

Symbols: circle, ring, rings intertwined, hexagon, doves, Shri yantra, #3

Rituals/Events: unity candle, handfasting cord

15. Nature based / Earth

Colors: green, blue, brown

Flowers/plants: moss, ivy, wildflowers, passionflower, dandelion

Herbs: arborvitae, sage, mugwort, kava kava

Crystals/gems: river stones, tree agate, moss agate, flourite, chrysocolla

Symbols: Gaia, crow, fairies, ancestors, tree of life, tree of knowledge, sacred grove, mushrooms, cypress tree

Timing/Direction: north, full moon, winter

Rituals/Events: honoring Gaia

To ensure cohesiveness, I would suggest sticking to only a few recognizable items of symbolism and weaving them into all of your pre and post handfasting events.

As we close this chapter on the rich tapestry of symbolism in handfasting ceremonies, it's evident that these rituals are more than mere formalities. They are imbued with meanings, which transcend physical acts, weaving together threads of history, culture, spirituality, and personal significance. Handfasting is not merely an exchange of vows or rings; it's a celebration of unity, a dance of balance between the individual and the collective, and a journey into the realms of tradition and personal expression.

The symbols used, whether ancient or modern, serve as powerful reminders of the interconnectedness of life, love, and community. As each couple embarks on this sacred journey, they are not only declaring their commitment to each other but also participating in a timeless ritual honoring the past, sanctifying the present, and looking forward with hope to the future. In embracing these symbols, they weave their own story into the enduring fabric of human experience, adding their unique thread to the ever-evolving narrative of love and connection.

Now that we've explored the rich world of symbolism, let's move on to another crucial aspect of your Pagan wedding: the vows. In the next chapter, we'll delve into the art of crafting custom vows, which truly reflect your unique love story and spiritual beliefs.

CHAPTER 10 CUSTOMIZING THE CEREMONY SCRIPT AND VOWS

Have you ever wondered what it would be like to express your love and commitment in your own words, rather than the traditional 'I do'? Unlike traditional weddings where vows often follow a set script, Pagan weddings offer the freedom to completely tailor the ceremony and vows. This open-ended nature allows for a pure expression of the heart and soul. The vows can be written in various forms – from poetic verses and storytelling to simple, heartfelt promises. Couples can get creative, perhaps incorporating song, art, or other expressive forms. Every relationship is unique, and custom vows highlight the specific bond the couple shares. They can speak to their unique quirks, shared passions, challenges they've overcome together, and the special ways they support and love each other.

In this chapter, I provide an outline of typical Pagan wedding vows, which you can customize, followed by some examples of wedding vows you may use or further customize.

Outline of Handfasting Ceremony

1. Procession:

The order of arrival of the wedding party as they enter the ceremony.

Customizations: Your wedding party may include the officiant, the groom, family members, bridesmaids and groomsmen, a ring bearer, horseshoe bearer, light bearer, flower child or feather child or symbolic participant. The order of arrival and timing can be changed, the music played can be customized and the places they stand or sit can be customized according to your plans or venue.

2. Opening by the Officiant:

- Welcome and introduction, acknowledging the significance of the occasion.
- Explanation of the meaning and traditions of handfasting.
- Invocation or prayer, calling upon the elements, deities, ancestors, or spirits.

Customizations: Consider examining the proposed introductory remarks provided by your officiant. They probably have a variety of options for you to choose from. Your spiritual practices may determine what is included in any invocation or prayer.

3. The Exchange of Vows:

- The officiant invites the couple to declare their vows.

- The couple takes turns reciting their personalized vows.

Customizations: Many couples write their own vows. Think about the journey you've shared, the challenges you've overcome, and the happy moments defining your relationship. These reflections can provide inspiration and authenticity to your vows. When designing your own vows, a clear declaration your love for each other is the foundation of your vows. Express your commitment to your partner, highlighting the permanence and depth of your relationship. Make promises which are meaningful and realistic, reflecting both the joys and the challenges in a relationship. You may acknowledge the qualities in your partner who you admire and love, and how they have impacted your life. You might mention your shared aspirations, how you plan to achieve them together, and your vision for the future.

While the vows should be personal, including some universal themes like love, commitment, and support can resonate with your guests and make the ceremony more inclusive. Poetry, art or other creative expression can be added either as part of the actual vows or as an additional element after the vows.

4. **Optional Unity Ritual** (e.g., Lighting a Unity Candle, Sand Pouring Ritual):

- Introduction of the unity ritual and its significance.
- The couple performs the unity ritual, like lighting a single candle from two individual ones, to symbolize the merging of their lives.

Customizations: The handfasting cord is a unity ritual in itself. However, some couples choose to customize their ceremony by adding an additional ritual. Here is a list of examples or you could make up your own.

Unity Candle Ritual:

Lighting a unity candle from two individual candles to symbolize the joining of two lives into one. The candles can be inscribed with symbols or runes for added significance.

Planting a Tree:

Planting a tree together during the ceremony, symbolizing the growth and nurturing of their relationship. The type of tree can be chosen for its spiritual significance.

Blending of Sands:

Pouring different colored sands into a single vessel, representing the coming together of two individuals to form a harmonious whole.

Water Ritual:

Pouring water from two separate vessels into one, symbolizing unity and the flow of life. Water from significant locations can be used for added meaning.
Jumping the Broom:

An old tradition symbolizing the sweeping away of the old and welcoming the new. The broom can be decorated with herbs, flowers, and ribbons.

Sharing of Mead or Wine:

Drinking from a shared cup as a symbol of their commitment to share all that life brings. Mead, in particular, has historical significance in many Pagan cultures.

Binding with an Oath Ring:

Placing their hands on an oath ring while saying their vows, an ancient tradition symbolizing the binding nature of their promises.

Elemental Blessing:

Incorporating blessings or actions representing the four elements (earth, air, fire, water), such as lighting a candle, burning incense, pouring earth or sand, and blessing with water.

Labyrinth Walk:

Walking a labyrinth together during the ceremony, symbolizing the journey of life with its twists and turns.

Cauldron Ritual:

Using a cauldron in the ritual to symbolize the womb of the Earth, adding ingredients symbolizing different aspects of their relationship and future life together.

5. Exchange of Rings:

- Blessing of the rings by the officiant.

- The couple exchanges rings, each partner placing a ring on the other's finger with accompanying words.

Customizations: You can customize the words said when the couple exchanges rings. Similar to the vows, this should reflect the couples values and the theme of the wedding. You could also add a rituals such as a ring warming ceremony, where the rings pass through the hands of all present before they are exchanged. This allows guest to imbue them with good wishes and blessings, involving the community directly in the nuptials. You can customize how the rings are provided. In some cases the rings are held by the best man and given to the groom. Other times, the officiant holds the rings. Or you could have a special ring bearer. That is one way to involve a child. You can make your own custom ring bearer pillow or have one custom made.

At the time of exchange of rings, you can also have a horseshoe bearer bring up a horseshoe shaped object (either an authentic horseshoe or one crafted from cloth with a handle to present to the bride, symbolizing luck. This is another way to involve children in the ceremony.

6. Handfasting Ritual:

- Explanation of the handfasting cord's symbolism by the officiant.
- The couple joins hands, and the officiant or a designated individual loosely drapes the cord over their hands, symbolically binding them.
- The officiant leads the couple through affirmations of their bond.

Customizations: You can customize your handfasting cord in the colors of your choice to match your theme. You can customize the number of strands braided into it, the material, the charms and craft one yourself and dedicate it in a separate ceremony. The words said by the officiant and the couple can be customized.

7. Pronouncement and Kiss:

- Presentation of the bride and groom
- Couple kisses

Customizations: The officiant pronouncement may be customized, and the style of kiss may be customized. You may choose to have other family members such as children of the couple join the couple for the pronouncement and have the pronouncement include declaring the family bond.

8. Unbinding of the Hands:

- The officiant unties or removes the handfasting cord, symbolizing ththe couple remains connected by their vows, yet free in their individuality.

9. Closing Remarks by the Officiant:

- Final blessings or wishes for the couple's future. Acknowledgment of the guests and thanksgiving for their presence and support.
- Instructions for the recessional or next steps in the celebration.

Customizations: You may choose to have the guests applaud, throw birdseed or lavender buds at the couple, greet the couple in a receiving line or otherwise close the ceremony.

Script Examples

The following are several examples of customized scripts for a general Pagan handfasting, a Viking style handfasting, and a Wiccan style handfasting for a couple with children.

Script #1 - General Pagan Handfasting

(Officiant stands at the altar, couple stands facing each other in front of the officiant.)

[Opening by the Officiant]
[Officiant]: "Welcome, friends, family, and honored guests. In the presence of the elements, under the open sky, and before the spirits who guide us, we gather here today to celebrate the union of [Partner 1] and [Partner 2] in the sacred rite of handfasting. They have chosen to bind their lives together, not by law or tradition alone but by their own love, trust, and commitment. Let the elements bear witness to their union. Let us invoke the blessings of the elements and the ancestors as we commence this sacred rite. May their love be as enduring as the earth, as constant as the cycles of the moon, and as passionate as the flames of the sacred fire."

[Officiant may lead a brief invocation or prayer, tailored to the couple's spiritual path or call in the elements as follows.]

[Calling of the Elements]

[Couple holds hands.]

[Officiant]: "We call upon the spirits of the North, the element of Earth, to bless this union with strength, stability, and abundance. May your love be as unwavering as the mountains, [[Partner 1] and [Partner 2], and may your commitment be as fertile as the Earth itself."

[Officiant]: "We call upon the spirits of the East, the element of Air, to bless this union with clear communication and understanding. May your words and thoughts always flow freely between you, [Partner 1] and [Partner 2], and may your love be as boundless as the sky."
[Officiant]: "We call upon the spirits of the South, the element of Fire, to bless this union with passion, creativity, and transformation. May your love burn brightly, [Partner 1] and [Partner 2], igniting your hearts with desire and your souls with inspiration."

[Officiant]: "We call upon the spirits of the West, the element of Water, to bless this union with love, emotion, and intuition. May your hearts always overflow with compassion and your love flow as freely as the rivers, [Partner 1] and [Partner 2]."

[Exchange of Vows]

[Officiant]: "Now, [Partner 1] and [Partner 2], please share the vows you have prepared, as a testament to your commitment and love for one another."

(Each partner takes turns reciting their vows. Partner 1 goes first, followed by Partner 2.)

[Partner 1]: "I promise to cherish, honor and respect you, not only on sunny days when our love shines brightly, but also on the stormy nights when darkness threatens. I vow to be more than your partner; I want to be your shelter, your refuge, your home. I pledge to love you without conditions, embracing every facet of your being, your light, and your shadow. With this hand, I offer you my heart, and in it, a love that will not waver, a love that will endure through every twist and turn of our journey through this world, and in all realms, for we are bound not only by the love between us but also by the sacred bonds of nature that connect us to the earth, the sky, and all living beings."

[Partner 2]: "I promise to cherish, honor and respect you, not only when life is a smooth and easy path but also when we stumble upon challenges testing our strength. I vow to be more than your partner; I want to be your confidant, your co-conspirator, your muse. I pledge to love you without boundaries, embracing your dreams as if they were my own and standing beside you in the face of adversity. With this hand, I offer you my heart, and within it, a love that knows no bounds, a love that will transcend time, and a love that will thrive for all eternity. As we bind our hearts together, may our love echo through all realms and reverberate through the tapestry of existence, honoring the sacred harmony of nature and the enduring bonds that connect us to all that is."

[Unity Ritual (example-Lighting a Unity Candle)]

[Officiant]: "This unity candle symbolizes the light of your individual selves coming together to light the path of your shared life. May its flame burn brightly and guide you through the years."
(The couple each takes their individual candles, which were lit before the ceremony, and together light the larger unity candle.)

[**Exchange of Rings**]

[Officiant]: "May these rings be blessed as the symbol of this affectionate unity. The rings are a testament to the couple's bond, as constant as the stars and as enduring as the mountains. With these rings, you encircle one another in the eternal symbol of your love."

[Partner 1]: "With this ring, I promise you my heart, my soul, and my spirit. For all my days I am yours."

(Partner 1 places the ring on Partner 2's finger.)

[Partner 2]: "With this ring, I promise you my heart, my soul, and my spirit. For all my days I am yours."

(Partner 2 places the ring on Partner 1's finger.)

[**Handfasting Ritual**]

[Officiant]: "The handfasting cord represents the binding together of your two lives."

(The officiant or a designated individual loosely drapes the handfasting cord over the couple's joined hands.)

[Officiant:] "Your hands are now bound, symbolizing that from this day forward, your lives are also bound. To affirm your commitment, do you [Partner 1] agree to be bound in sacred union to [Partner 2]?"

[Partner 1:] "I do."

[Officiant:] "Your hands are now bound, symbolizing that from this day forward, your lives are also bound. To affirm your commitment, do you [Partner 2] agree to be bound in sacred union to [Partner 1]?"
[Partner 2:] "I do."

[Officiant:] "As the cord is tightened, so is your bond strengthened. As it holds you together, may your love hold you in its embrace, and may you find in each other the greatest of joys and the truest of companions. These two lives are now joined in one unbroken circle, bound together by mutual trust. Wherever they go, may they always return to one another in their togetherness. May they forever shine as a testament to the vows you have shared today."

[**Pronouncement and Kiss**] Officiant: "By the power vested in me and by the strength of your own love, I pronounce you [partners, spouses, husband and wife, etc.]. You may seal your vows with a kiss."

(The couple shares a kiss.)

[**Unbinding of the Hands**]

[Officiant]: "May your love be forever blessed, [Partner 1] and [Partner 2]. As this cord is unbound, may your love remain unbroken. Though bound to each other, remember to keep one another in the space to grow, breathe, and be yourselves. May this cord remind you always of the ties that bind you together, and the love that sets you free."

(The officiant removes the handfasting cord.)

[Closing Remarks by the Officiant]

[Officiant]: "May your love so endure that its flame remains a guiding light unto you. We thank the elements, ancestors, and all who have joined us today. Go now in peace and love, sharing the joy of this union with all whom you meet."

(Officiant offers final blessings.)

[Recessional]

[Officiant]: "Ladies and gentlemen, I present to you [Partner 1] and [Partner 2] in their new journey together. Let us celebrate their union!"

(The couple then leads the recessional, walking down the aisle together, followed by their wedding party and guests. Music or a traditional song plays as they exit.)

Script #2 - Viking Handfasting Ceremony

[Opening by the Officiant]

[Officiian]t: "We gather in the spirit of the ancient Norse, under the open sky, to witness the handfasting of [Partner 1] and [Partner 2]. In the presence of the old gods and the mighty spirits of this land, we invoke the blessings of Odin, Freya, and Thor on this union."

[Invocation. The officiant raises their hands or holds a ritual object such as a staff or a wand, signaling the beginning of the invocation.]

Officiant: "Great spirits of the earth, sky, and sea, we gather here in your magnificent presence to witness and bless the union of [Partner 1] and [Partner 2].

We call upon the ancient and mighty Norse gods to bestow their blessings upon this couple.

Odin, Allfather, wise and far-seeing, grant them the wisdom to navigate the journey of their life together.

Freya, goddess of love and beauty, bless their union with love as enduring as the stars and as deep as the ocean's heart.

Thor, protector and guardian, lend them your strength to weather the storms they may face and the courage to fight for their love and happiness.

We also call upon the spirits of nature – the steadfast mountains, the deep and mysterious forests, the rushing rivers, and the vast, open skies. Let the steadfastness of the earth, the freedom of the air, the passion of the fire, and the adaptability of the water infuse their relationship with balance and harmony.

May the ancient energies of this land and the wisdom of the gods guide and protect [Partner 1] and [Partner 2] on their sacred journey of love, companionship, and mutual growth.

In this sacred space, with the blessings of the gods and the ancient spirits, let the vows made today resonate through the realms, witnessed by the elements and nurtured by the love that surrounds us all.

So may it be."

[The officiant lowers their hands or ritual object, signifying the end of the invocation.]

[Exchange of Vows]

[Officiant]: "[Partner 1] and [Partner 2], as you stand before the gods and this assembly, speak now your vows to each other."

[Partner 1:] "Before the gods and all gathered here, I, [Partner 1], pledge myself to you, [Partner 2]. Like the steadfast oak in the wild forest, I vow to be your strength; like the enduring fjords, my love for you is deep and unyielding. In the spirit of the mighty Viking warriors, I promise to protect you, to honor our family, and to face every adventure and challenge at your side. Together, may we ride the winds of life as fiercely and bravely as the Valkyries ride to Valhalla."

[Partner 2:] "In the sight of the gods and our kin, I, [Partner 2], give myself to you, [Partner 1]. As the resilient wolf roams the wild lands, so will I be loyal and devoted to you.

Like the ever-flowing mead in Valhalla, my love for you will never cease. I vow to stand with you, to weave our destinies together like the Norns weave the fates, and to cherish the life and family we build. May our journey be as epic as the sagas, filled with courage, love, and honor."

[Unity Ritual (Drinking from the Shared Horn)]

[Officiant]: "Now, share this mead as a symbol of the life you will share. Just as two streams come together to form a mighty river, so too will your lives now flow together into one unbreakable current."

(The couple each takes their individual horn, fills the larger horn with mead, and then drinks from the shared horn in turn, symbolizing unity and shared life.)

[Handfasting Ritual]

[Officiant]: "As your hands are bound together by this cord, so are your lives now entwined. May your union be as strong as iron and as lasting as the ancient mountains."

[The officiant or a designated individual binds the couple's hands together with the handfasting cord.]

[Pronouncement and Kiss]

[Officiant]: "By the power of the gods and the love you have declared, I pronounce you bound in the sacred tradition of our ancestors. You may now seal your vows with a kiss."

[The couple shares a kiss.]

[Closing Remarks by the Officiant]

[Officiant]: "Let the strength of your wills bind you together, let the power of love and trust make you inseparable, and may your days be long and prosperous. Skål!"

[The officiant raises their hands towards the couple, signaling the imparting of blessings.]

[Officiant]: "Under the eternal gaze of the heavens and the enduring strength of the earth, we close this sacred ceremony with the blessings of the old Norse gods.

May Odin grant you wisdom on your journey together, wisdom as deep as Mimir's well, guiding you through challenges and enriching your shared experiences.

May Freya's blessing of love and fertility be upon you, enveloping your union in passion, understanding, and a love as vast as the seas.

May Thor's might protect you, his hammer Mjölnir be your shield against adversities, and his strength fortify the bond you have forged today.

Let the steadfastness of the mountains inspire your commitment, the breadth of the skies expand your dreams, and the richness of the earth nurture your life together.

As the tree Yggdrasil connects all the worlds, so may your lives be intertwined, growing stronger and reaching higher, rooted in love and reaching for the stars.

We invoke the spirits of your ancestors, asking them to watch over you, guide you, and bless you with their wisdom. May they walk beside you, their presence a comforting shadow in your sunlit path.

By the elements and by the gods, your union is blessed. May you walk boldly and joyously into your shared destiny, knowing the gods smile upon you this day.

Skål! To [Partner 1] and [Partner 2], may your love and happiness echo through the nine worlds. So may it be."

[The officiant lowers their hands, signaling the end of the blessings.]

[Presentation of Couple]Officiant: "I now present to you [Partner 1] and [Partner 2], handfasted in the ways of the old. May their lives be as legendary as the heroes of old."

[The couple then leads the recessional, walking down the aisle together, possibly to the sound of traditional Viking music or drumming.]

Script #3 Wiccan Handfasting for Couple with Children

[Opening by the Officiant]

[Officiant]: "Blessed be! We are gathered within this sacred circle to celebrate the handfasting of [Partner 1] and [Partner 2]. In the presence of the elements and the divine, we honor the love, which has grown, and the family that has blossomed."

[Invocation]

[Officiant]: "Beloved spirits of the Earth, Air, Fire, and Water, we call upon your energies to surround us and infuse this space with your sacred essence. We stand upon the Earth, beneath the Sky, encircled by the nurturing arms of nature, as we witness the union of [Partner 1] and [Partner 2].

Great Goddess, Mother of the Moon and the Earth, who brings forth life and nurtures all creation, bless this union with your love and wisdom. Grace us with your divine presence, and imbue this ceremony with your nurturing touch.

Mighty God, Father of the Sun and the wild, protector and guide, bestow upon this couple your strength and courage. As the oak stands firm and the stag roams free, so too may their love be steadfast and their spirits indomitable.

Spirits of the North, guardians of the Earth, lend your stability and endurance. Spirits of the East, keepers of the Air, grant your wisdom and inspiration. Spirits of the South, masters of Fire, ignite passion and vitality within them. Spirits of the West, watchers of the Water, flow through them with love and intuition.

As we stand in this sacred circle, let the elements converge to bless [Partner 1] and [Partner 2] on their journey together. May their love grow, flourish, and withstand the test of time, as eternal as the cycle of seasons and as bountiful as the Earth itself.

So mote it be."

[Exchange of Vows]

[Officiant]: "In the divine presence, [Partner 1] and [Partner 2], please share your vows."

[Partner 1]: "Before the watchful eyes of the Goddess and God, under the endless sky and upon the nurturing earth, I, [Partner 1], join my heart and soul with yours, [Partner 2]. In the presence of the elements, our dearest ones, and our cherished children, I vow to be your partner in all things.

Like the oak tree, may our love grow strong and unwavering; like the gentle breeze, may our love be a constant and soothing presence. I promise to walk with you in light and in darkness, through the changing seasons of life, with unwavering faith, respect, and devotion.

To our children, [Children's Names], I vow to be a guiding light and a steadfast protector. I promise to nurture our family with love, patience, and kindness, weaving our lives together in a tapestry of joy and understanding.

As we stand handfasted, bound by love and trust, I pledge to honor the sacredness of our bond, to cherish and respect you, to support and inspire you, as we walk this path together, blessed by the Divine."

[Partner 2]: "In the circle of love and light, surrounded by the ancient energies of the earth and sky, I, [Partner 2], take you, [Partner 1], as my beloved. With the blessings of the Goddess and God, and in the sight of our family and our precious children, I offer you my heart, my soul, and my spirit.

Like the endless cycle of the moon, may our love be ever-renewing; like the depth of the seas, may it be profound and unyielding. I vow to journey beside you through life's mysteries, sharing in joy and sorrow, in triumph and challenge.

To our beautiful children, [Children's Names], I promise to be a source of love, wisdom, and strength. Together, we will build a home filled with laughter, learning, and compassion, honoring the unique light within each of us.

As our hands are joined in this ancient rite, I commit to you my deepest loyalty and affection. I vow to respect and cherish you, to grow with you in mind and spirit, hand in hand, heart to heart, as we forge our path guided by love and the blessings of the Divine."

[Family Unity Ritual]

[Officiant]: "Let us now celebrate the unity of this family. [Children's Names], please come forward to participate in blending the elements."
[Each child adds an element to the cauldron – earth for stability, water for emotion, air for intellect, and fire for passion, symbolizing the unity and balance of the family. The couple then adds wine to the cauldron, symbolizing the blending of all elements in their shared life.]

[Officiant]: "As these elements combine, so does this family unite in strength, love, and harmony. May you grow together, supporting and nurturing each other."

[Handfasting Ritual]

[Officiant]: "As your hands are joined by this cord, so too are your lives. May your bond be as strong and adaptable as the sacred knot before us."

[Handfasting cord is wrapped around the couple's hands.]

[Pronouncement and Kiss]

[Officiant]: "By the power of the Goddess and the God, I pronounce you not only as partners in life but as a united family under the stars. Seal this union with a kiss."

[The couple shares a kiss, followed by a group embrace with their children.]

[Closing Remarks and Family Pronouncement]

[Officiant]: "May the Goddess and the God bless [Partner 1], [Partner 2], and their children, [Children's Names]. Walk together in light and love, strengthened by the bonds of family. Blessed be your journey ahead!
Under the ever-watchful eyes of the Goddess and the God, with the blessings of Earth, Air, Fire, and Water, we have witnessed the sacred union of [Partner 1] and [Partner 2]. May their love be as eternal as the circle surrounding us, as deep as the roots of the earth, and as boundless as the skies above.

May the Goddess bless you with her abundance and nurture you with her compassion. May the God empower you with his vitality and protect you with his strength.

As you step forward into your shared path, may the elements guide you — the stability of Earth, the communication of Air, the passion of Fire, and the adaptability of Water.

May your home be filled with laughter, your hearts with joy, and your days with love. May you grow together, learn together, and cherish each moment of this journey you embark upon today.

And now, as we close this sacred circle, let us remember that, while the circle is open, it remains unbroken. The love and energy we have raised here today continue to resonate in our hearts and in the world around us.

By the power of the Goddess and the God, by the unity of Earth, Air, Fire, and Water, I declare this sacred space closed. Go now in peace and love, carrying the blessings of this day with you. So mote it be."

[The officiant makes a closing gesture, often walking around the circle or waving their wand or athame to symbolically cut the circle, releasing the energy while maintaining its protection and blessings.]

[Presentation of Couple and Recessional]

[Officiant]: "I present to you the newly united family: [Partner 1], [Partner 2], and their children. May their path be ever guided by love and unity.

Now that you have a better understanding of how to create your own custom vows, let's move on to Part 3 Crafting Your Dream Ceremony where we will bring it all together into a cohesive plan for spectacular chain of events and learn to avoid common pitfalls.

PART 3: CRAFTING YOUR DREAM CEREMONY

CHAPTER 11 MASTERING THE ART OF SACRED UNION

Do you know how to kick-start planning the handfasting event of your dreams? Perhaps you are familiar with all of the options and order of events, or maybe it's your first time learning about the events leading up to a handfasting ceremony. Thus far, you have been given a glimpse into various handfasting customs, traditions and rituals. But how do you take these components and weave them together into a cohesive chain of events within your budget? This chapter explores the main options for ordering the events and discusses how you can customize and integrate these rituals into your chain of events. You have a unique circumstance. Be confident there is a solution.

My partner and I were brimming with excitement and eager to get married right away. However, our friends and family were located in other states, making it a challenge to gather everyone in one place. It would take months to plan and organize the unforgettable, epic wedding event we envisioned. How could we have both a swift marriage and a spectacular event? Our day had to be special. I wanted to have a ceremony, which reflected our personalities, featured customized vows and incorporated certain rituals. We did not want to simply sign a paper in front of the justice of the peace in a government office. We found a cost-effective solution which allowed us to have two special wedding days! Now the only question remaining is which one should we celebrate as our anniversary day? I will spill the beans on our romantic solution in a moment.

Handfasting Celebration Events

Let's review the primary types of events related to a handfasting celebration. Think of this as a flexible buffet of events, where you have the freedom to choose or discard as you wish. The sequence of these events is also adjustable to suit your needs. Every element carries a specific cost. It also requires careful planning and execution. This responsibility often falls on the couple, a wedding planner, or their family and friends. Therefore, consider your available resources, such as budget, time frame, venue sizes and the time commitment and cost commitment of those involved.

Event Line Up

1. Request for Blessing/Permission from Parents
2. Marriage Proposal
3. Family Dinner Announcement
4. Engagement Party
5. Bridal Shower or Bachelorette Party/ Bachelor Party/ Same-Sex Pre-Marital Party
6. Handfasting Rehearsal
7. Handfasting Ceremony
8. Handfasting Reception
9. Honeymoon
10. House Blessing and/or House Warming

The handfasting ceremony (#7) may be further broken down into its typical elements:

Part 1 Pre-ceremony preparation

    A. Site preparation
    B. Dressing of the couple
    C. Guest arrival and attunement

Part 2 Ceremony

    A. Grand entry
    B. Officiant Opening Words
    C. Officiant casts the circle / blesses ceremony
    D. Officiant performs ceremony and consecrates rings
    E. Couple exchanges vows and rings
    F. Couple unity ritual
    G. Officiant ties handfasting cord
    H. Officiant pronounces marriage
    I. Officiant uncasts circle

Part 3 Post-ceremony

    A. Receiving line
    B. Offerings on altar

For each occasion, you will need to define the order of events and rituals you want to include. The above order can be changed to fit your needs. You will need to know necessary aspects: the budget, date, venue, host, list of guests to be invited, event facilitator or officiant, preferred attire, seating, communication plan. You must make decisions on optional aspects: theme, decorations, flowers, music, food and beverage, cakes, rituals and ritual tools, gifts, guest favors, photography and videography. You will also need to know the amount of lead time you need in advance to order or reserve each of goods/services. For instance, you may need to reserve a particular venue six months to a year in advance. A custom cake may have a lead time of 2-4 weeks.

The level of complexity varies by event. Certain events you select may not require a substantial number of elements. You can look for packages from event venues with many of the elements included or referrals for some of the services. Planning from scratch can indeed seem daunting and overwhelming.

We will delve into each of these event categories to better understand the origins and purposes of them. Before we proceed, here is the reveal of the creative solution we found to my own wedding conundrum.

My partner and I, who live in the Houston, Texas area, chose to elope to San Antonio, Texas, a 3-hour drive from Houston. We found an inexpensive elopement package online, which included the wedding officiant, flowers and a photographer/witness. We chose the River Walk, an elegant location with a spot called Marriage Island, which is a little patch of land in the river showcasing a huge oak tree. We were able to customize the vows, bouquet and some of the ceremony elements. We decided to make the date St. Patrick's Day because of our Irish heritage and the big celebration on River Walk when they dye the river green and have a boat parade.

I wore a fairly inexpensive green and gold gown for the occasion, styled my own hair and embellished my hair clips with matching jewels for the occasion. I crafted and blessed our themed handfasting cord in advance, and the officiant graciously tied the cord uniting us in marriage. As it happened, our ceremony became a grand spectacle, drawing in a large audience of passersby. Even strangers dining on a nearby restaurant balcony joined in the celebration, cheering us on with great enthusiasm and toasting our sacred union.

Although simple, it was truly a memorable event, special for the two of us. I am grateful for the intimate, romantic moments we were able to share, just the two of us, without the need to divide our attention amongst friends and family in the whirlwind of a grand wedding and reception. We spent the rest of the day celebrating on the River Walk. Several individuals who had the privilege of witnessing the event extended their sincere and warm congratulations.

The event was of minimal cost. We stayed at an AirBnB cottage instead of a River Walk hotel to save money. Then we still had the rest of the year to plan our big, medieval-style handfasting in November at the Renaissance Festival with every part customized. We do celebrate our anniversary on March 17 as that was the day we were officially joined in sacred union.

Even the simple elopement required the signing of contracts and some amount of pre-planning. You can use a spreadsheet to stay organized, listing out each aspect of the trip and ceremony, costs, contract dates, contact names, basically the who, what, where and how of the event. On my website, you can download free templates for planning KatSticker.com/downloads.

Handfasting Ceremony Events Further Defined

Request for Blessing/Permission from Parents

Why might adults feel the need to seek permission to marry? This practice has deep roots in history. Arranged marriages were a common occurrence in many ancient and medieval societies where parents were pivotal in the selection of a life partner. It was a common practice for parents or other family members to negotiate and orchestrate marriages on behalf of their children. Marriages were frequently viewed as alliances between families, tribes, or communities, with parents playing a significant role in choosing a suitable spouse for their children. In some Western societies, the Enlightenment era and the Industrial Revolution instigated changes in social and economic structures. As the concepts of individualism and romantic love gained prominence, there was a gradual shift away from strictly arranged marriages. Even in regions where arranged marriages are still common, there has been a noticeable trend towards greater autonomy and choice for individuals in choosing their life partners.

In Western cultures today, many contemporary couples inform their parents about their decision to marry and seek their blessings rather than formal permission. The continuation of this tradition may be rooted in the romanticism of the practice in films. The tradition of asking for parental blessing to marry has been a sentimental element in many films over the years. Filmmakers often use this practice to add emotional depth and tension to the plot and to highlight themes of love, commitment, and family approval.

Take your relationship with your parents and your family's traditions into consideration to determine whether this practice makes sense for you. If you do decide to ask for blessings, you could arrange for a formal blessing ceremony in your parents' home with one or both sets of parents present.

<u>Marriage Proposal</u>

Imagine proposing through a scavenger hunt where your partner finds clues which lead to the proposal. Or perhaps you organize a flash mob with friends to surprise your partner with a choreographed dance or performance ending with your proposal. Consider using a cinema's marquee or screen to display a custom message before a movie. These wacky, fun proposal ideas are commonplace. You can customize the proposal to your hobbies and interests and be as public or private with the moment as you desire.

You may wish to incorporate rituals with oaths and promises in your proposal where both partners make commitments to each other and your families. Additionally, many proposers may present an engagement ring at the time of the proposal symbolizing their commitment to their partner.

<u>Family Dinner Announcement or Engagement Party Illustration</u>

Back in the day, popping the question was a whole fancy affair! For instance, Celtic society placed a significant emphasis on community and the participation of the community in important life events. It is likely that marriage proposals and engagements were witnessed and celebrated by the community with feasting, music, and celebration. Gift-giving was an important part of Celtic culture, and it likely played a role in marriage proposals. It is possible that the exchange of gifts between families or between the prospective bride and groom symbolized the formalization of the marriage agreement. The following illustrative story shows what a handfasting engagement might have been like.

In the heart of a bustling Celtic village, nestled between rolling hills and winding rivers, lived a young and ardent warrior named Aiden. Aiden had been deeply in love with Saoirse, the daughter of the village's wise elder, for as long as he could remember. He longed to make her his bride and build a life filled with love, laughter, and adventure. Saoirse had been told by her parents that a union with Aiden would bring their families closer in an important alliance. Saoirse did not know if she would like being married to Aiden but she imagined it often in her daydreams.

One bright spring morning, with the sun's golden rays painting the landscape, Aiden decided it was time to ask Saoirse for her hand in marriage. But in Celtic society, popping the question was no ordinary affair. It was a grand celebration of love and unity. Aiden began his preparations by crafting a splendid oak wood necklace, adorned with intricately carved symbols representing their shared dreams and aspirations. This necklace would be his token of love and devotion. Next, he sought the counsel of his closest friends, who were eager to help orchestrate the perfect proposal.

As the day of the proposal approached, the entire village buzzed with excitement. Aiden's friends secretly arranged for musicians to serenade the village square with melodies that resonated with love and joy. The aroma of savory stews and freshly baked bread filled the air as villagers gathered to witness the grand event.

Aiden, dressed in his finest attire, stood at the center of the square, his heart pounding with anticipation. Saoirse, radiant in her Celtic gown adorned with wildflowers, entered the square, accompanied by her father, the village elder. The moment was finally here. With a flourish, Aiden presented the exquisitely carved oak wood necklace to Saoirse. Tears of joy glistened in her eyes as she accepted the token of his love. The villagers erupted in cheers, clapping and singing songs of love and unity. Aiden and Saoirse embraced, their hearts entwined, their love celebrated by all.

And so, in the heart of the Celtic village, under the watchful eyes of their community, Aiden and Saoirse embarked on their journey of love, guided by the traditions of their ancestors and the warmth of their village's embrace.

Today, we see less of families being involved in the marriage proposal and more in the celebration after the proposal is accepted. When a couple becomes engaged, they may wish to announce it at an intimate family gathering or hold a larger engagement party with family and friends or both. If you don't have it in your budget to do an engagement party and a reception after the wedding, choose to invest in the reception. More people expect a reception than an engagement event. If you want to have both, but still lack sufficient budget, try spacing them out to budget over a longer period of time.

A gathering such as this is a wonderful time to incorporate rituals related to commitment and blessings for fertility and abundance. You might choose a cacao ceremony, fire blessing, or tree planting, all described in Chapter 8.

Bridal Shower or Bachelorette Party

From dazzling parties to thoughtful presents, it's all about making the bride feel truly exceptional. A bridal shower is a daytime event focused on giving gifts and celebrating the bride's upcoming marriage in a more traditional and relaxed setting, often with female family members. A bachelorette party, on the other hand, is probably an evening or night event focused on celebrating the bride's last days of singlehood with entertainment and fun activities, often with friends and bridesmaids. Both events serve as opportunities to show love and support for the bride in different ways.

Samantha was getting married, and her best friend, Emily, was determined to give her the perfect pre-wedding celebrations. She knew that Samantha would appreciate both a traditional bridal shower and a lively bachelorette party. So, Emily decided to plan two distinct events which would cater to Samantha's different sides.

A Bridal Shower Tale

Emily rented a garden venue for Samantha's bridal shower, inviting her close family and friends. The venue was decorated with flowers and vintage items, and classical music played softly. The highlight of the shower was a "kitchen gadgets game" where guests identified kitchen tools while blindfolded. Samantha, in a white sundress, opened gifts of cookware, dinnerware, and a personalized apron. Emily had prepared a heartfelt toast, sharing stories of their friendship and wishing Samantha all the happiness in the world. Tears welled up in Samantha's eyes as she thanked everyone for their love and support. Finally, Emily had prepared a blessing bath ritual Samantha where the guests added herbs and flowers to her water and she purified herself for the wedding.

A Bachelorette Party Tale

A week later, it was time for Samantha's bachelorette party. Emily had rented a stylish limousine and gathered Samantha's spirited group of friends. They started the evening with a visit to a trendy karaoke bar where Samantha belted out her favorite songs. The laughter was infectious, and the night was still young.

The next stop was a lively nightclub, complete with flashing lights and a live DJ. Samantha wore a sash, which read "Bride-to-Be" and a veil with blinking LED lights. She danced the night away with her friends, making unforgettable memories. The group indulged in a late-night pizza outing, giggling and sharing stories about Samantha's dating adventures before she met her soon-to-be husband.

Finally, they lit a bonfire and cheered on Samantha as she tossed her little black book of men's phone numbers into the flames to symbolize her commitment to her betrothed.

Bachelor Party

While it's true that men love a good party, the evolution of the bachelor party is a tale as old as time, weaving through the annals of history from the raucous celebrations of ancient Rome to the hearty festivities of medieval Europe. But it's in the modern age that this pre-wedding tradition truly found its stride. Today, bachelor parties are often seen as a way for the groom and their friends to bond and celebrate the groom's last moments of singledom before entering married life. The specific activities and style of bachelor parties can vary widely, from quiet gatherings to extravagant trips and adventures.

Same-Sex Premarital Party

Same-sex couples celebrate bachelorette and bachelor parties with a few variations and considerations which reflect their preferences and identities. Ultimately, the most important aspect of bachelorette and bachelor parties is personalization. Same-sex couples can create celebrations reflecting their unique personalities, interests, and preferences, like any other couple. There are no set rules for how same-sex couples should celebrate their pre-wedding festivities. The key is to create a memorable and enjoyable experience aligning with the couple's wishes and the preferences of their friends and guests.

Handfasting Rehearsal

Practice makes perfect! The more complexity to the ceremony and larger the group of couple's attendants (all of the people involved in the ceremony), the more important the rehearsal becomes. Even in the simple elopement I experienced at the Riverwalk, we held a rehearsal to walk-through the parts of the ceremony. It is not necessary to dress in the wedding day attire for a rehearsal. Likewise, it is not necessary to actually light candles or perform any ceremony rituals at the rehearsal. You can simply pretend to light the candles; pretend to pour the water or anoint with oil, etc. That keeps the sacred elements intact for your real ceremony.

If the rehearsal is a day in advance of the ceremony, the rehearsal may include a rehearsal dinner immediately following the ceremony rehearsal. The couple's attendants and sometimes their parents are invited to this dinner. If a dinner is within your budget, it is another opportunity for the couple to receive a toast / blessings or other ritual.

Handfasting Ceremony

Site Preparation: Check with your venue how much time you have for the complete ceremony including setup and take down of decorations. Your package with the venue may include set up of seating arrangement. However, the wedding party normally decorates the venue. Make a list what items you need to bring and how you will transport them to the venue from your vehicle. For instance, you may have chair covers, flowers, handfasting altar, guest register and more. Everything should be organized in advance so nothing is left behind and it is easily set up. A checklist is handy to keep track of the items and who is responsible for bring them.

You may also want to clear or cleanse the space with ritual herbal smoke or spritz with essential oils and water. Unless the building of your handfasting altar will be part of the ceremony, this is another ritual you can do in advance if you are planning to have a handfasting altar.

Guest Arrival and Attunement: As handfasting ceremony guests arrive, you may have a hostess greet them, hand them a program of events and invite them to sign a wedding register to show that they attended the wedding. The register then becomes keep-sake memorabilia for the couple. If you have many guests, you may want to assign ushers to help them find seats. In some traditions, the bride's family and friends sit on one side of the aisle whereas the groom's family and friends sit on the other side of the aisle. Consider reserving some seats up front for VIP guests, such as the parents of the couple.

 Attunement of the audience releases any negative energy and may be a ritual to include here. Either the officiant or another facilitator trained in attunements can perform the ritual. The facilitator will introduce the attunement to the guests and explain its purpose, which is to create a moment of harmony, connection, and energetic alignment among everyone present. A description of this ritual is in Chapter 8.

Grand Entry: A procession of handfasting attendants parades to the front of the venue and stand in pre-assigned spots. The couple may enter together, or the bride may come after the groom being delivered to the groom's side by a close family member who symbolically "gives the bride away" to the groom. You can adjust the order to your values, traditions and number of people in your procession.

This is a good opportunity to include children of the couple in the ceremony as attendants or to carry important symbols. For instance, my step-son was bearer of the horseshoe, a friend's daughter was light-bearer (carrying a lantern), my son was a ring-bearer and my daughter carried a basket of feathers. She was supposed to hand feathers to guests on the edges of the aisle but was so nervous, she did not give away any feathers. You have to expect children may not carry out their duties as intended. They may be confused about what to do or nervous about being "on-stage." It is a big day for them as well.

Officiant Opening Words: The officiant welcomes the couple and their guests, acknowledges any special guests, family members, or deities which the couple wishes to honor. The officiant acknowledges the sacredness of the moment and sets the intention for the ceremony as a celebration of love and unity. They provide a brief explanation of the handfasting ritual, its historical significance, and its representation of binding love and commitment. And they may cover any other script that the couple requests such as the symbolism of certain rituals to be in the ceremony or any parts the guest may be expected to perform.

Casting of the Circle and Blessing: Many Pagan ceremonies, including handfastings, begin with the casting of the circle and calling of the directions. Ensure you have an officiant who is comfortable and knowledgeable about how to do this. It creates a sacred and protected space for the ceremony and acknowledges the energies associated with the four cardinal directions (North, East, South, West) and sometimes the elements (Earth, Air, Fire, Water). The officiant may also call on ancestors, spirits, goddesses or other correspondences for blessing the couple and the ceremony. The process is described in Chapter 8.

Consecration of Rings: The consecration of rings is a meaningful ritual in many handfasting ceremonies where the officiant blesses the rings and imbues them with positive energy, intention, and symbolism. The officiant may purify the rings with incense smoke or call in a deity to bless them.

Vows and Rings: In the next part of the ceremony, the couple exchanges vows and rings. The couple may write their own vows or choose from pre-written vows provided by the officiant. Most officiants allow the couple to edit and adjust the vows to their own needs. Each partner places the ring on the ring finger of their betrothed. This is customizable if you don't want to exchange rings but prefer to exchange another object symbolic of your commitment. Before or after the vows is a good time to insert a song or poem customized for your union.

Unity Rituals: After the vows and before the handfasting cord is a good time to do unity rituals. It may be difficult to do a unity ritual after the handfasting ritual because your hands are tied together. You could also place the unity ritual before the vows or after the handfasting cord is released or during the reception. The main purpose of a unity ritual in a handfasting ceremony is to symbolize the coming together and union of two individuals into a single, harmonious partnership. For example, the couple may chose to light a unity candle. Each person holds a candle representing their individual self and lights the main unity candle symbolizing family. Children of the couple may join in this one with their own candles. It helps them to understand the significance of the moment.

Another tradition is jumping the broom or "besom." A broom is placed on the ground and a couple jumps over it to symbolize leaving single life behind and jumping into marriage.

Another popular unity ritual is pouring different colors of sand into a glass vase, mixing the colors together. This is another ritual in which children can easily participate.

Some ideas for non-traditional unity rituals include creating art together, stepping inside a circle of love made of flowers or stones, which represents the universe encompassing their relationship, or building a small cairn (stack of stones) during the ceremony. Each stone represents an aspect of their relationship or a hope for their future, symbolizing the building of their life together on a solid foundation.

Handfasting Cord: This ritual involves the officiant binding the couple's hands together with a cord or ribbon, symbolizing their union, commitment, and the joining of their lives. The couple may be asked to extend their right hands, left hands, or both, depending on tradition and preference. As each wrap of the cord is made, the officiant may share words of symbolism and intention. For example: The first wrap represents the couple's past, their individual lives before coming together. The second wrap symbolizes the present, their commitment and union in the here and now. The third wrap signifies the future, the journey they will embark on together. Make sure your cord is long enough for the wrapping and tying in advance!

In some cases, the handfasting cord ritual is done before the vows and rings and sometimes afterwards. It is up to the couple to decide the order of events you prefer. Using a family heirloom, such as a piece of vintage cloth or a family quilt, to bind the couple's hands during the handfasting ritual, adds a layer of family heritage and continuity to the ceremony. You can also braid your own handfasting cord using 3 ribbons and attaching some symbolic charms. The handfasting cord is a lifelong keepsake, which makes a beautiful display for your home.

Pronouncement of Marriage: The officiant declares the couple married. The couple traditionally will kiss in front of the guests at this point. The kiss serves as a physical symbol of the couple's commitment to each other and public declaration of their union. It is a way to seal the vows they exchanged, signifying their mutual consent and affection.

Uncast the Circle: The officiant gives any closing remarks. Then they uncast the circle by reversing directions and thank the directions, elements, any deities invited and the guests.

Receiving Line: After the couple and handfasting attendants exiting procession, the couple and sometimes their parents, children line up. The guests greet and shake everyone's hands as they exit the venue.

Offerings on Altar: The couple may give offerings on their handfasting altar before and/or after the ceremony and may or may not invite guests to give offerings, such as flower or grain. If guests are invited to make offerings, the couple may provide a bowl of offerings for the guests to use because it is unlikely guests brought an offering with them. It would be impolite to ask the guests to leave money on the altar.

Handfasting Reception

Receptions are held directly after the handfasting ceremony, in most cases, and may last several hours. The wedding and reception may take place at the same venue, or the reception may be held at a different location. Be sure the guests are aware of the location of the reception in advance and the time frame it will be held. Similar to the handfasting ceremony, the couple needs to plan how long they have to decorate and undecorate the space and set up the seating. Normally the venue sets up the seating arrangements and allows advance decoration of the venue. Receptions are a celebration after the handfasting and may include feasting, dancing, gifts and other rituals, such as a toast to the couple. At the end of the reception, there may be a "sending off" of the couple to their wedded life with tossing of birdseed or lavender buds or bubbles, depending on what the venue allows.

Honeymoon

Couples might desire to embark on their marital journey with a honeymoon getaway providing them with an intimate and romantic seclusion, allowing them to revel in their newfound wedded bliss. Rituals may enhance the honeymoon experience, giving deeper meaning to the time spent together.

House Blessing and/or House Warming

A house warming party normally occurs in the home of the newlyweds if they are just moving in together with their close friends and family. Guests bring gifts and get to see the home. Sometimes a meal or party food is served. You may choose to incorporate a house clearing and blessing into the house warming party or hold it as a separate event. A house blessing may be performed by an officiant or by the couple themselves throughout the home they will share during their marriage. Some couples clear and bless their home annually. This ritual is often completely customizable.

Budget Considerations

If you are on a tight budget, there are some easy ways you can cut down costs. First, you can skip the pre-ceremony events such as engagement party, bridal shower, bachelor and bachelorette parties, and rehearsal dinner. You may still need a rehearsal to take place, but not hold a dinner afterwards. In fact, if your ceremony is brief, you can hold the rehearsal the same day as the event. You can also cut out post-handfasting events such as the honeymoon and house warming party.

It is not recommended to eliminate the handfasting reception, unless it is an elopement. Guests expect a reception, even if it is a budget-friendly reception. Ways to cut the budget on the handfasting ceremony and reception is reduce the number of guests invited, hold it at someone's house or an inexpensive venue, play your own music instead of hiring a DJ or band, get help from family for providing food and a cake instead of having it catered, eliminate alcohol from the event, cut down on the amount of decorations and flowers or make your own decorations and handfasting cord. You could also repurpose a gown you already have as a wedding gown or use a hand me down dress.Think Do it Yourself (DIY) and simplification to the extent possible. The amount of DIY you have time to do may depend on the size and willingness of your inner circle to step up and help. DIY may also require additional time to prepare and keeping track of the DIY items on a checklist is critical. As your inner circle is not under contract, may not be experienced, and may not be compensated to make the decorations, bake the cake, provide their backyard for the event, they are less likely to perform these activities on schedule and to the level of quality as a business. Therefore, be careful in assigning DIY items to friends and family, taking into consideration their skill set and reliability.

Know how much money you have to spend before you start looking at venues and planning your guest list. In some cases, family members may contribute to your financial resources. Confirm that before you spend too much time on planning the events. Start with planning the budget for the most critical events, such as the ceremony and reception. Then plan the pre- and post-handfasting events with any budget left over. Obtain quotes from multiple vendors to compare prices. List out all of the options with prices for each aspect of the event before committing. This ensures you have flexibility to choose or eliminate different options to build your own package and ensure the total cost is affordable.

Look for wedding package offerings that can save you money. Some venues may have a package including most of the aspects of the ceremony and reception, which can save money over obtaining from separate vendors. The venue may also be able to recommend a list of vendors for things like the DJ, cake, photography, etc. Ask your friends for budget-friendly recommendations as well. They may have attended an amazing wedding and be able to put you in touch with good vendors.

Resources

What is the best wedding experience you have ever seen? Whether it was a wedding you attended in person or watched in a movie, what were the elements that made it over the top for you? List those out. Now were some of the worst wedding experiences you witnessed? List out the elements that you want to avoid.

In planning your handfasting chain of events, you can either create your own spreadsheet, or download a free Handfasting Planning Kit from my website: www.ritualshouse.com/downloads. The kit is a zip file including a Handfasting Event Planner Template, Handfasting Order of Events, Budget Planner, Ritual Planner and much more.

CHAPTER 12 THE POWER OF
YOUR INNER CIRCLE

Introduction to the Inner Circle of Participants

In the sacred tradition of handfasting, the inner circle is not merely a gathering of loved ones; it's a vibrant tapestry woven from the threads of ancient wisdom and modern bonds. Much like the Druids of old, who under the moonlit skies formed circles of unity and trust, today's handfasting ceremonies call upon a similar circle. This inner circle, comprised of family, friends, and spiritual guides, plays a pivotal role in not only supporting the couple but also in amplifying the spiritual essence of the ceremony.

You can and should call on this same type of inner circle power for the planning of your handfasting events. If you have a few people who can help you with the event, it is going to save you time, effort and stress in rolling out a sequence of events. This chapter covers the roles of your wedding party and how they are valuable assets. Keep in mind, all is customizable for your needs. You could elope without any of the inner circle. Involving others can build your bonds with family, friends and community as they will feel honored that you want them to participate. Modern, diverse family structures and non-traditional roles can be adapted in a handfasting ceremony to accommodate the couple's unique circumstances and make it inclusive for everyone.

The Couple at the Helm

At the forefront of these sacred rites is the betrothed couple, the architects of their journey. Their role goes beyond mere planning; it involves blending ancient traditions with personal significance. Each decision they make, such as choosing the color of the handfasting cords or selecting melodies for the ceremony, reflects their unique love story. They stand not as solitary planners but as leaders of a shared vision, weaving the advice of elders with their aspirations to create a ceremony resonating with timeless significance. Their leadership in planning is not about dictating each element; rather, it's about orchestrating a symphony of personal and shared visions. They carefully consider the traditions which speak to their hearts, weaving them with innovative ideas symbolizing their journey. Every choice, from the color of the handfasting cords to the melodies floating through the air, is a reflection of their story and aspirations.

In this journey, the couple often becomes the confluence point where ancient traditions meet contemporary desires. They listen to the advice of elders, peers and family, blending it with their intuition and preferences to create a ceremony, whichis both timeless and personal. Their role as leaders is marked by a balance of respect for tradition and a bold embrace of individuality. This leadership extends to collaborating with their inner circle, the officiant, and various vendors. They share their vision, forging alliances with those who understand and respect the sanctity of their ceremony. Through this process, the couple not only crafts an event celebrating their union but also embarks on a journey of growth, learning the art of compromise, communication, and joint decision-making. Ultimately, the couple's leadership in planning their handfasting ceremony is a profound exercise in shared creation.

Bridesmaids and Groomsmen

A couple may choose to involve one or more bridesmaids to support the bride and one or more groomsmen to support the groom during the planning process as well as to participate in the ceremony. The bridesmaids and groomsmen emerge as more than participants; they are the bedrock of support. Rooted in protective traditions, their roles have evolved into being confidants, advisors, and the emotional backbone for the couple.

They partake in rituals, infusing the ceremony with communal strength and love. Their presence is a living testament to the couple's journey, a blend of shared memories and future promises. They may hold important ceremonial items. For example, a bridesmaid may hold the brides bouquet or horseshoe during the handfasting ritual.

 They may assist in the handfasting ritual itself. For instance, one or more groomsmen may cast the sacred circle, symbolizing the community's embrace and protection of the couple. Each bridesmaid or groomsman may offer blessings and readings. Prior to the handfasting ceremony, the bridesmaids may plan and execute a bridal shower and/or bachelorette party or other pre-handfasting ceremony rituals to honor the bride. The groomsmen may plan and execute a bachelor party or other pre-handfasting ceremony rituals to honor the groom. Or they may plan together pre-handfasting ceremony dinners to honor the couple such as an engagement party or dinner.

Maid of Honor and Best Man: Leading with Heart

One bridesmaid may be chosen as a maid or matron of honor to have a lead role amongst the bridesmaids and have the largest supporting role during the handfasting ceremony. Similarly, one groomsman may be chosen as a best man to lead the groomsmen and act as the main facilitator for the groom in the handfasting ceremony. Their roles are imbued with responsibility and affection, guiding pre-ceremony rituals, and standing as the chief supporters during the ceremony. As their roles are very important and may be time consuming, the couple traditionally provides bridesmaids and groomsmen with a small gift as a token of their appreciation.

The Officiant as the Facilitator

The officiant stands as the guardian of traditions and the weaver of the sacred space. They guide the ceremony with wisdom, blending Pagan traditions with the couple's story. Their role is to create a spiritual environment where the couple's union is celebrated not just in a physical realm but in a cosmic sense. A handfasting officiant's responsibilities include:

- Crafting a ceremony aligning with the couple's spiritual path and personal story.

- Facilitating the flow of the ceremony, including guiding the couple and guests through rituals.

- Creating and maintaining a sacred space conducive to spiritual and emotional depth.

- Ensuring the legal aspects of the marriage (if applicable) are fulfilled.

Close Family and Loved Ones

In Pagan handfasting events, the involvement of close family members and loved ones goes beyond mere attendance; they play integral roles intertwined with the spiritual fabric of the ceremony. Their blessings, support, and presence within the sacred circle are vital contributions which enhance the sanctity and significance of the event.

Parents and Elders: Parents and elders often play a significant role, sometimes participating in specific rituals. In some cases, the bride's father, brother or uncle may be asked for permission to marry prior to the engagement and may walk the bride down the aisle at the handfasting ceremony.

They may be involved in the lighting of unity candles, offering of gifts, or the blessing of the couple during the handfasting ceremony or the reception. They may have the lead in making a toast to the couple or kicking off any of the events leading up to or after the handfasting. They may host the engagement party or rehearsal dinner or may pay for the ceremony cost. If paying for a substantial amount of the event or events, the parents may want to have a significant role in deciding on the event agenda and details. Their involvement is a nod to the continuity of family lineage and tradition, as well as an acknowledgment of the wisdom and guidance they provide.

Siblings and Close Relatives: Siblings and close relatives can serve as bridesmaids and groomsmen or fill more practical roles, providing support and assistance during the series of events.   They may help with preparations such as decorations, food, making arrangements, sending invitations, seating guests or other checklist items. They may participate in rituals, such as readings, singing, or assisting in setting up the sacred space.

Children of the couple: If the couple has children, they can play special roles, symbolizing the blending of families. They might participate in the ceremony by carrying symbolic items, such as flowers, crystals, or elements of the handfasting ritual itself.

Extended Family Members: Extended family members (aunts, uncles, cousins, grandparents, etc.) often contribute by being part of the sacred circle, symbolizing the community's embrace. They might also help with organizational aspects or contribute to the ceremony with music, art, or storytelling, depending on their closeness to the family.

Significance of the Circle

Blessings and Emotional Support

The presence of family and loved ones serves as a profound source of emotional strength for the couple. Their blessings, both spoken and unspoken, infuse the ceremony with love and positive energy, reinforcing the couple's commitment. In many traditions, family members may offer blessings or words of wisdom, either formally during the ceremony or informally in the celebrations that follow.

Spiritual and Community Connection

The inclusion of family and loved ones is a testament to the interconnectedness of individual journeys. Their presence symbolizes the wider community's acceptance and support of the union, reinforcing the couple's role within the broader spiritual and social fabric.

Cultural Variations

The specific roles and involvement of family members can vary widely depending on cultural backgrounds, individual family traditions, and the couple's preferences. Some ceremonies might incorporate more traditional roles, while others could be more contemporary or personalized.

In conclusion, the involvement of close family members and loved ones in a Pagan handfasting ceremony is a beautiful blend of tradition, emotional support, and spiritual significance. Their roles, whether ceremonial or supportive, contribute immensely to the depth and richness of the ceremony, echoing the timeless adage that a wedding is not just a union of two individuals, but the coming together of families and communities.

Energy of the Inner Circle The inner circle is more than a collection of individuals. Each person embodies a unique energy and connection, contributing to a rich tapestry of spiritual and emotional resonance that defines the atmosphere of the ceremony. Each participant in the sacred circle represents a unique energy and connection. Each participant's energy is shaped by their personal relationship with the couple, their own experiences, and their intentions for being part of the ceremony.

The circle has no beginning and no end, symbolizing the eternal nature of the love and commitment being celebrated. The intentions and blessings of the inner circle are important, acting as spiritual affirmations for the couple's future. The collective intent of all participants can amplify the ceremony's significance. When spoken or held in thought, they weave a supportive network of positive energy, manifesting a collective wish for the couple's happiness, prosperity, and well-being. Therefore, it is critical to create a supportive and loving environment within the inner circle.

Offer guidance on fostering positive energy and intentions among participants. Be a gatekeeper to exclude disruptors to this sacred energy. Do not be a disruptor yourself. When you put forth negative energy because a level of perfection is not achieved at your event, which erodes the energy and atmosphere of your event and the trust of the participants. Better to go with the flow and accept that some imperfections can make your event unique and memorable.

Choose Your Inner Circle Wisely

The composition of your inner circle is a crucial aspect of your handfasting preparations, influenced by various factors such as the scale of your pre- and post-ceremony events, the guest list size, your budget, the complexity of the rituals, and the availability of potential participants. When selecting your inner circle, prioritize long-term relationships to ensure a harmonious atmosphere. It's important to balance inclusivity with the practicality of managing dynamics. You want to avoid feelings of exclusion, which could impact longstanding relationships. But it's equally vital to steer clear of including individuals whose presence might be disruptive or toxic.

In situations where a potential participant's reliability is a concern, consider assigning them a role with less critical responsibility. Flexibility is key in forming your inner circle. Remember, it's perfectly acceptable to have an uneven number of bridesmaids and groomsmen or to break traditional gender roles in your selection. The aim is to create a circle that resonates with your values and vision for the ceremony, rather than adhering rigidly to conventional expectations. In essence, mold your ceremony to fit your unique circumstances and relationships, rather than forcing conformity to traditional norms.

Embrace and celebrate the power of your chosen inner circle. The interconnectedness of all participants in the sacred journey of the handfasting can last well beyond the related events bonding your circle together even closer for the future

CHAPTER 13 RISK MANAGEMENT AND OTHER PLANNING CONSIDERATIONS

Imagine you have the most amazing handfasting timeline planned. You hand-made the decorations, wrote your vows, planned magical, transformative rituals, landed a beautiful location for the ceremony and reception. Everything is proceeding according to plan. After the event you begin receiving criticism from friends and family about certain details, which while magical, are not aligned with your commitment to earth conservation practices. The butterflies you had planned to release mostly were dead on arrival. *Cringe.* The rice you planned for guests to throw turned out to be hazardous to wildlife. *Oops.* You did not have a plan for trash removal and plastic refuse was released into the environment. *Sorry.* You planted a tree without permission from the venue and now have to pay for its removal. *Uggh.* Aunt Eva was accidentally left off the guest list and has now disowned you. *Wow.* The caterer was an hour late for the reception, and everyone was hungry. *Mercy.* And your officiant did not file the paperwork, so you are not actually legally married. *Arrrgh.*

What could go wrong? That is the question you should ask yourself before finalizing the details of your handfasting timeline.

Risk management is an important part of each and every event planning process. Reducing your risks of illegal acts, vendor non-performance or quality issues, disappointed guests, miscommunications, health and safety hazards, and failure of your plan in general is crucial to your success in running your dream handfasting event. Additionally, you want to make sure you are not overspending your budget. This chapter brings awareness to some of the major concerns you should address in your handfasting timeline of events.

I am not listing the legal requirements for each possible jurisdiction. Laws and regulations change. If I list out the current requirements for marriage in your state, the law could change after the publication of this book and you could have the wrong information. There is no way I could keep up with all of the rules for each place. For instance, details about residency or citizenship requirements, waiting periods between obtaining the license and ceremony, required documents beyond identification are many details, which could vary from place to place. Also, I am not an attorney.

You must perform your own research for your locality. That goes for laws for the other items in this chapter as well. For example, there may be a temporary burn ban due to a drought in your city preventing you from having a bonfire. There is no way I could know about that. The reason I focus on risk management - what is most likely to go wrong with the highest consequences - is so that you know what you need to independently confirm for your particular circumstance.

1.   Legal Requirements for Marriage

In the United States, couples typically need to obtain a marriage license from the local county or city clerk's office. The requirements for obtaining a marriage license can vary by state and sometimes even by county. Generally, both parties must appear in person and provide valid identification, such as a driver's license or passport. Some states may require proof of residency or citizenship. Many states have a waiting period between obtaining the marriage license and the actual ceremony. The waiting period can range from a few hours to several days, depending on the state. However, some states allow couples to waive the waiting period under certain circumstances, like completing premarital counseling. As stated above, you should contact your local government to learn the requirements for your particular jurisdiction.

In Canada, couples normally need to obtain a marriage license from a local government office or municipal clerk's office in the province or territory where you plan to marry. Both parties may need to appear in person to apply for the license. Valid identification, such as passports or birth certificates, may be required. There may be a waiting period between obtaining the license and the marriage ceremony, but this varies by province. Marriage ceremonies can be performed by authorized officials, including judges, justices of the peace, religious leaders, and registered civil marriage commissioners.

Requirements for marriage licenses in Europe vary significantly from one country to another. In some European countries, couples must give notice of their intention to marry at a local registry office or town hall, which is often done several weeks or months in advance. This notice is usually published publicly to allow for any legal objections. Many European countries have waiting periods between the notice of intent to marry and the actual ceremony. This waiting period can range from a few days to several weeks.

Marriage licenses in Mexico are issued by the local civil registry office (Registro Civil) or the municipality where you intend to marry. Both parties will generally need to provide valid identification (such as passports) and proof of marital status (e.g., divorce decree or death certificate if previously married). Blood tests may be required in some states. Most Mexican states require at least two witnesses, often with valid identification, to be present during the ceremony. Civil ceremonies in Mexico are typically performed by a judge or an authorized official at the civil registry office. Religious ceremonies may be performed by clergy members, but it's important to ensure the marriage is registered with the civil authorities to be legally recognized.

The legal requirements for marriage in other countries can be quite diverse and may depend on local laws, customs, and religious practices. Some countries may have strict requirements, while others may have relatively straightforward processes. It's essential for couples planning to marry in a foreign country to research and understand the specific requirements and regulations of that country, which may include documentation, waiting periods, and officiant qualifications.

2.   Officiants and Legal Recognition

Non-recognized clergy are individuals who are not officially authorized by the state or government to perform marriage ceremonies. This may include individuals who have become ordained online or through organizations which do not have formal recognition as religious institutions. Marriages officiated by non-recognized clergy may not be legally valid, depending on local laws and regulations.

In the U.S., officiants who can solemnize marriages include judges, justices of the peace, ministers, priests, and other religious leaders. The rules for who can officiate a marriage ceremony can vary by state, and some states may allow friends or family members to become ordained for the purpose of officiating a wedding.

In Europe, officiants may include government officials, judges, mayors, or authorized civil celebrants. Religious weddings are also common, and they are often performed by clergy members in a religious institution. The requirements for who can officiate a marriage ceremony can vary by country and may depend on whether the ceremony is civil or religious.

It's essential to research the specific marriage laws and regulations in your jurisdiction to determine who is considered a recognized officiant. In many cases, recognized clergy have the authority to solemnize both civil and religious marriages, while non-recognized clergy may only be able to perform religious ceremonies which are not legally binding.

3.   Marriage Documentation

After your ceremony, the officiant must fill out paperwork. The officiant, along with the couple and witnesses, must complete and sign the marriage license that was issued previously. The marriage license is a legal document which records the essential details of the marriage, including the names of the couple, the date and location of the ceremony, the names of the witnesses, and the officiant's signature.

In many jurisdictions, the officiant is responsible for ensuring that the completed and signed marriage license is returned to the local county or city clerk's office for official recording. The timeline for returning the marriage license can vary by location, so it's important to check with the issuing authority for the specific requirements and deadlines.

After the marriage license is recorded by the clerk's office, the couple can request certified copies of their marriage certificate for legal and personal use (e.g., for name changes, immigration purposes, or insurance). The process for obtaining certified copies also varies by jurisdiction, and there may be associated fees.

It's essential to check with the specific county or city clerk's office in the jurisdiction where you plan to marry for any unique requirements or variations in the process.

4.   Insurance and Liability
Planning a wedding involves various insurance and liability considerations to protect against unexpected events or

accidents. Here are some types of insurance and liability coverage you may want to consider for your wedding:

- Wedding Liability Insurance:

Event liability insurance can protect you against financial losses resulting from accidents or incidents occuring during your wedding. This coverage can help cover costs if someone is injured, or property is damaged during the event. It can also provide protection in case of unexpected issues with vendors, like a caterer not showing up or a venue canceling.

- Cancellation or Postponement Insurance:

This type of insurance can provide coverage if you need to cancel or postpone your wedding due to unforeseen circumstances, such as severe weather, illness, or a vendor's failure to deliver services. It can reimburse you for non-recoverable expenses, helping you reschedule or recoup costs.

- Travel Insurance:

If you're planning a destination wedding or if you and your guests are traveling from afar, travel insurance can provide coverage for trip cancellations, lost luggage, medical emergencies, and other travel-related issues. If you're having a destination wedding, consider event insurance which covers issues specific to international or destination events, like travel disruptions or local regulations.

- Rental Insurance:

If you're renting items such as tents, tables, chairs, or decor, rental insurance can protect you in case these items are damaged, stolen, or don't arrive as expected.

- Vendor Insurance:

Some vendors, such as caterers or transportation providers, may carry their own liability insurance. Verify their coverage and ask for proof to ensure you're not held liable for any issues related to their services.

- Liquor Liability Insurance:

If you plan to serve alcohol at your wedding, consider liquor liability insurance. This can provide coverage if a guest becomes intoxicated and causes harm or accidents.

- Health and Liability Insurance for Participants in Physical Activities

If your wedding includes physical activities like sports or adventure activities, consider liability insurance to protect against injuries or accidents.

When considering these insurance options, it's essential to read policy terms and conditions carefully, understand coverage limits, deductibles, and exclusions, and compare quotes from different insurance providers to find the best coverage for your needs. Consulting with an insurance professional can also be helpful in making informed decisions about your wedding insurance and liability needs.

5.   Contracts with the Venue and Vendors

You need written contracts with any vendors or service providers for your event and you should read the entire contract. Ask questions about anything you do not understand before you sign it. Confirm your understanding of the basics or any important details. Get referrals or references for your vendors and check that they have a good reputation. Understand their policy about payment due dates and refund circumstances. Know the capacity limits of the venue before inviting 1000 people. Verify the timeframe you have access to the venue to set up and decorate and clean up so you can plan ahead. They may have another event planned directly before or after yours with no leeway for running over on time. The venue and or city zoning could have restrictions on certain ritual components, such as fire, animals, hazardous materials, noise, or serving alcohol. Don't assume anything. Reconfirm the vendor services even after having a written contract.

6.   Waste Management

Who is cleaning up after your event? If you are renting a venue, the venue may state in the contract that you are responsible for cleaning up and disposing of trash or the venue may do it. Be sure you know in advance. If you are not renting a venue, but having it at Aunt Sally's house, do not assume Aunt Sally is cleaning up afterwards. Clarify who is cleaning up or Aunt Sally may be quite angry when you leave a big mess. She might assume you are making arrangements to clean up afterwards. Be sure you keep trash contained during the event if you are outdoors, so that bottles and plastic do not end up inadvertently left in the woods.

7.   Ritual Components or Hazards

If you are planning fire, candles, fireworks, smoke or any toxic materials to use in a ritual or special effect, take care that (1) the venue allows it and (2) you have safety measures in place in case of an accident. Fire extinguishers, ventilation, cordoned off area to protect children are some examples of safety measures to plan. Of course, it depends on your specific circumstance and use case. You need to have a backup plan in case there is a burn ban in effect at the time of your event. The key to not stressing out at event time is planning ahead for contingencies.

8.   Animals

I caution against using live animals for rituals or special moments because (1) it is difficult to predict animal behavior, (2) your reputation is at stake and (3) there is so much that can go wrong.

Some guests or wedding participants may hold the opinion that any use of animals as exploitation of the animal, especially when Pagans are very connected to nature and environmental concerns. If anything bad happens to the animal(s) during your event, that will be the one thing the guests remember and talk about, and they will likely blame you. Not all animal handlers act responsibility or kindly with their animals. Please ensure you use a handler with a stellar reputation if you choose to have animals.

Consider any safety hazards caused by dangerous animals. Check on venue restrictions with regard to having animals in the venue and city ordinances with restrictions on live animal events. Do all of the checking before booking any animal acts.

If you want to bring your own pet to an event, make sure you have someone designated to take care of the pet at the event. If you are one of the wedding participants, you will likely be busy at the event and not able to hold a dog or cat the whole time. Pets can experience anxiety and fear at overwhelming events, especially if it is a large affair or they are not used to strangers or crowds. Make sure the situation will be safe physically and emotionally for your pet.

CHAPTER 14 WEAVING THE FUTURE: BEYOND THE HANDFASTING

In summary, the purpose of a handfasting ceremony is primarily to symbolize the binding together of two people in a commitment akin to marriage. Originating from ancient Celtic traditions, handfasting involves the literal tying of the couple's hands together with cords or ribbons. This act represents the couple's intention to join their lives together. Handfasting can be either a stand-alone ceremony or part of a larger string of wedding celebration events. It emphasizes unity, commitment, and the start of a new journey together as partners. This ritual is adaptable to various spiritual and personal beliefs, making it a versatile and meaningful choice for many couples.

Reflection and Appreciation

After your beautiful event is over, you may feel a moment of letdown with the thrill of planning festivities behind you. You may suddenly experience anxiety about the future since there is more time to think on it. This is the perfect time to reflect on the handfasting ceremony and cherish the moments that went right. Discuss the significance and personal meaning of the ceremony with your partner and your inner circle. Acknowledge and express gratitude to friends, family, officiants and community who were involved.

Be sure to encapsulate the journey from planning to living the handfasting experience through a scrapbook or other mementos which are true keepsakes. You may preserve your bouquet, gown, handfasting cord or other ceremonial items to display or showcase your event.

Embarking on a Journey of Reflection and Gratitude

As the echoes of your enchanting ceremony fade, it's common to feel a sense of longing as the excitement of planning settles into memory. You may suddenly experience anxiety about the future since there is more time to think on it. Take heart as you find yourself at the threshold of a new adventure.

Embrace this moment as an opportunity for reflection and gratitude. Picture each moment of your handfasting ceremony as a precious gem, sparkling with personal significance. Share these treasures with your partner and inner circle, igniting conversations about the magic of that day. Extend your heartfelt thanks to the cast of characters - friends, family, officiants, and community - who played a role in your tale. Recognize and honor the unique contributions of each participant especially those in your inner circle.

Craft a Tapestry of Memories

Your handfasting journey, rich in detail and emotion, deserves to be chronicled. Create a scrapbook or a treasure chest of mementos - your bouquet, gown, the handfasting cord - each a chapter in your story, waiting to be revisited and celebrated.

Write Your Epic Saga Together

Your grand ceremony has concluded, but the quest you've embarked on with your partner is eternal. Now begins the thrilling task of charting your path forward. Discover new ways to nurture your bond and strengthen your relationship post-ceremony. Together, you'll craft a life filled with love, challenges, and triumphs. How will you weave the vows and promises of your handfasting into the fabric of your everyday lives? Remember, the unending knot is not only a symbol; it's a map of your ongoing journey, a guide for navigating life's twists and turns as a unified force.

Celebrating the Seasons of Your Saga

Your handfasting was a landmark, but many more festivities await on the horizon. Anniversaries, birthdays, and holidays become milestones in your ongoing adventure. Now is the perfect time to envision new traditions, blending the mystique of Pagan rituals with the joy of personal celebrations. As your family grows and evolves, these traditions become the heartbeat of your shared journey, enriching your spiritual connection and binding your story together.

You may want to start new family traditions or incorporate other rituals and ceremonies into celebratory moments. This may help you deepen your spiritual practices as a couple. You can explore further Pagan rituals and traditions. As your family grows, consider how to involve children, pets and extended family and community.

Charting Your Course: Resources for the Road Ahead

To aid you in your journey, visit KatSticker.com/downloads for an arsenal of handfasting planning tools. The Handfasting Planning Kit is your compass, complete with checklists, planners, and timelines, guiding you through the mystical landscape of ritual design. The Rituals House blog is a treasure trove of knowledge, offering insights into the art of ritual practice.

A Blessing for Your Voyage

As you step forward into your shared future, may your handfasting be the dawn of a lifetime filled with love, growth, and endless adventure. May your journey together be as boundless and beautiful as the unending knot you've tied.

Recommended Additional Reading

"Ancient Ways: Reclaiming the Pagan Tradition" by Pauline Campanelli

"Pagan Heart of the West Embodying Ancient Beliefs and Practices from Antiquity to the Present: II. Nature and Rites" by Randy P Conner

ABOUT THE AUTHOR

Kat Sticker is an artist, author and energetic healing practitioner. She lives on the Texas Gulf Coast with her husband, two talented children and a slew of fur babies. Kat is a trained herbalist, certified in several Reiki modalities, Akashic Records reader, trained in several Shamanic energy healing techniques, elemental alchemist and ritual designer. Her mission is to share her light codes to make joy, wisdom, wellness, harmony and abundance more accessible to those seeking a spirit-led life.